Jack the Myth

JACK the MYTH

A New Look at the Ripper

A.P. WOLF

ROBERT HALE · LONDON

First published in Great Britain 1993

ISBN 0 7090 5151 4

Robert Hale Limited
Clerkenwell House
Clerkenwell Green
London EC1R 0HT

2 4 6 8 10 9 7 5 3 1

Photoset in Palatino by
Derek Doyle & Associates, Mold, Clwyd.
Printed in Great Britain by
St Edmundsbury Press Ltd, Bury St Edmunds, Suffolk.
Bound by WBC Bookbinders Ltd, Bridgend, Mid-Glamorgan.

Contents

It's a very funny thought
that, if Bears were Bees,
They'd build their nests
at the bottom of trees.
And that being so (If the
Bees were Bears)
We shouldn't have to
climb up all those stairs.

Illustrations

Between pages 88 and 89

Acknowledgements

Thanks are due to the publishers of the following books for permission to include extracts: *Winnie the Pooh* by A.A. Milne published by Methuen Children's Books, *Alone with the Devil* by Ronald Markham and Dominick Bosco published by Piatkus Books, and *Jack the Ripper A–Z* by Begg, Fido and Skinner published by Headline Books.

Preface

It is baffling that some of the finest crime writers of our century have busied themselves for years with the horrific crimes committed in Whitechapel in 1888 by Jack the Ripper, and in reality have not come one inch closer to the identification of the killer or his obscure motives. In fact it is no exaggeration to say that we are now, over one hundred years later, further away from the truth of the matter than ever before.

The majority of 'Ripper' writers are responsible for this sad and confusing situation, for it is they who have portrayed the killer as some kind of superhuman monster. Almost the Invisible Man claims one famous writer on the subject[1] – capable of deadly acts bordering on the supernatural, striking out at will against harmless prostitutes with terrifying force and speed. A black-caped demon clutching a black bag full of horrors and capped with a deerstalker, prowling the darkened streets of Whitechapel, dismembering and disembowelling – in one case almost utterly destroying his victim beyond all recognition – when he will, how he will, and without let or hindrance from a helpless and seemingly immature police force.

1 Jack the Ripper

A name to chill the blood, an elusive black wraith of murder and mayhem who still eludes, deludes and fascinates us today. That is the image we are constantly given by some authors and it is these same authors who have, to a certain extent, been guilty of mystifying and magnifying the case of Jack the Ripper out of all proportion to what was really a serious murder inquiry. To their credit some of them may well have captured the soul and the spirit of Jack the Ripper, but in doing so they have irretrievably lost their man. They have concentrated on the myth and so enlarged it that the man disappears from the pages of history and we are left grappling with a character from fiction much like Count Dracula or Frankenstein.

Ripper literature has evolved over the years into some kind of super-pornography, designed to titilate the discerning reader – the sophisticated armchair murderer – with much, much more than standard pornography can ever offer, with its elaborate theories of forbidden sex and bodily destruction. To take but one lurid example which has the impotent killer substituting his penis for a knife and then thrusting it into the reproductive organs of his victims as an act of sexual finality.[2]

The details of the horrific murders are mulled over in a serious crime-writer style of language as is appropriate to this peculiar form of high-class pornography, but the sexual connotations which probably sell the books in the first place are still there. For example:

Was Mary Jane Kelly buggered before being ripped to pieces?[3]

Did the Ripper cut the throats of his prostitute victims while they were bent over in front of him exposing their backside for sex or did he lay them on the ground, have them raise their skirts for sexual intercourse and then plunge his knife into them?[4]

Even Donald Rumblelow – a policeman who is considered to be the leading authority on the Ripper murders – in his otherwise serious examination of the case *The Complete Jack the Ripper* couldn't resist the temptation to inform his readers that the killer most likely struck from behind as most prostitutes in those days preferred anal intercourse rather than normal intercourse to prevent unwanted pregnancies. He then goes on to reveal that the majority of prostitutes are able to bring a man to climax without any insertion at all, merely grasping the offending object between their thighs to satisfy their customer. One is left wondering exactly what these choice snippets concerning the sexual behaviour of prostitutes in 1888 and today have to do with a murder case, and where the author gleaned his astonishing information from in the first place? Perhaps Rumbelow could explain to his readers why he chose to include in his book horrifying pictures of the bloody remains of the victims of the Ripper?

It is well worth looking at some of Colin Wilson's comments in his latest effort – as he is one of the most prolific Ripper writers of all time – to come to grips with *his* Ripper. In describing the Ripper about his task of killing Annie Chapman Wilson equates the killer's behaviour with that of a dog copulating with a bitch on heat.[5] Mary Jane Kelly's murder has blood spurting over walls and Wilson postulates that the Ripper must therefore have been naked when he discovered the 'ultimate thrill', a 3-month-old foetus in the victim's womb.[6] When it comes to Catherine Eddowes murder Wilson uses words like 'delight' and 'delicate' to describe the horrifying attack and then goes on to make the curious statement that the killer 'went almost insane' when he found another victim to murder and mutilate.[7] That is an odd way to describe the actions of a knife-wielding maniac with a bent for murdering and then cutting the insides out of women.

Surely the Ripper was *already* insane before he began his attack on Catherine Eddowes? In the case of Annie Chapman's sad and brutal murder Wilson's choice of words is particularly painful. After all what on earth have copulating dogs got to do with the callous murder of a woman? And Wilson's 'ultimate thrill' of the Ripper discovering the foetus of a child in the womb of Mary Jane Kelly is a bit of a damp squib. Dr Thomas Bond's extensive post-mortem carried out the day after Kelly was murdered makes it absolutely clear that she was *not* pregnant. There was no foetus to provide Wilson's Ripper with the ultimate thrill.

As an aside to the main story Colin Wilson throws in a case where the victim's intestines were torn out through her vagina, and keen to show us that his Ripper is no ordinary mass murderer he launches into a dramatic and bloody description of the Ripper at his gruesome work. He reveals that the Ripper was not content merely to stab and maim his victims but achieved his pleasure from delving into the bodies and extracting the bloody contents.[8] He then goes on with what almost seems admiration for his Ripper when he describes the killer as being as skilful as a butcher who would never have left a woman dying and performed his mutilations by touch alone.

We will have much more to say about Wilson's opinions and his general influence on the subject of murder, past and present, later, but for now this illustrates the 'stuff' that is the 'Ripperologist's' bread and butter. This is the type of fictional trivia that is constantly dished up in ever-increasing portions by people. Armchair detectives writing about the activities of the Ripper for their specialized readers, armchair murderers. In this curious and unique literary vacuum the roles become strangely reversed with the armchair murderers becoming the helpless victims of their armchair detectives and crime writers.

Claims and counter claims fly back and forth between the various protagonists because they do not like it when their much vaunted theories are challenged. For instance if one author relates the rumour that sperm was found in the anal passage of Mary Jane Kelly, then it is immediately shot down by another because it ruins his own well-thought-out theory that the Ripper was unable to achieve an erection and used his knife instead. Anyone viewing the horrific photograph showing the little that remained of Mary Jane Kelly after her murder will immediately realize that this sort of question is academic anyway. Once again if the original post-mortem report is read it is obvious that such questions are firmly rooted in the minds of the 'Ripperologists' and not in reality. Dr Thomas Bond makes no mention in either of his two extensive reports of any signs of sexual contact.[9]

And while this serious scientific analysis and discussion goes on and on, concerning buggery and questions such as 'is it easier to slit the throat of a woman you are about to have sex with when she has her back or her front to you?', Jack the Ripper ducks and darts down the dark alleys of Whitechapel laughing his head off. Getting further and further away from his would be armchair pursuers while they compare notes about intestines being ripped out of vaginas and ask whether Jack the Ripper was really the Duke of Clarence, a secret Russian agent or even a black magician bent on creating a murderous pentagram to achieve the 'supreme power', whatever that is. It is a pathetic situation that has only grown worse as time has gone by, and will probably not improve in the future if one of the latest volumes on the 'Ripper' is anything to go by, where the following are all paraded before us as possible Jack the Rippers:

King Edward VII

Prince Albert Victor Christian Edward, Duke of Clarence

Lord Salisbury, Prime Minister

Right Honourable William Ewart Gladstone, Prime Minister

Lord Randolph Henry Spencer Churchill, Statesman

Sir William Withey Gull, Queen Victoria's physician

Dr Thomas Barnardo, founder of Barnardo's Homes

Helen Petrovna Blavatsky, founder of the Theosophical Society

Frank Miles, Royal Academy artist

A midwife[10]

It is worth mentioning that *all* these eminent Victorian public figures have been – and in some cases still are – considered serious candidates for the role of the 'Ripper' by various writers. A more than ample demonstration of the fantasy that has been created over the last hundred years by the 'Ripperologists'. The recently published *A to Z of Jack the Ripper* by Begg, Fido and Skinner is an admirable book amongst this deluge of fantasy, as it does stick to the factual information, but even so the book doesn't dismiss the fantasy entirely. For in a discussion of Stephen Knight's book *The Final Solution*, the authors say: 'In the end there is not a single piece of solid historical evidence adduced to support the sensational and controversial elements of Mr Sickert's [upon which Knight based his book] story. Nonetheless Stephen Knight holds a honoured place in the annals of Ripper research.'

For those who are not familiar with Knight's story it is based upon the premise that Prince Albert Victor had married a Catholic prostitute who was carrying his child.

This was known to a small group of Whitechapel prostitutes who attempted to blackmail the government and consequently Lord Salisbury, the prime minister of the day, set out to murder these prostitutes with the help of fellow Freemason Sir William Gull, Queen Victoria's physician-in-ordinary. It is a marvellous piece of fiction but does not stand up to a critical examination of its facts. Particularly in regard to Annie Elizabeth Crook – grandmother of Knight's informer, Joseph Sickert – the supposed Catholic wife of Prince Albert Victor and mother of his child. Most importantly it has been shown that Annie Elizabeth Crook was not a Catholic and if she had been then the marriage between herself and Prince Albert Victor would have been null and void under the Royal Marriages Act of 1772. Therefore it was not really necessary for Lord Salisbury and other high-ranking Freemasons to start murdering a gang of Whitechapel prostitutes. There are even more serious flaws to Knight's story, his attempts to link the mutilations carried out on the prostitutes with Freemasonry ritual are woefully inadequate and he was very selective with the facts he chose to use to back up his story. When the facts are carefully analysed it can be seen that Stephen Knight wrote his book around his theory and not around the facts, but this still allows him, according to the authors of the *A to Z of Jack the Ripper* a place of honour amongst the Ripperologists. So it seems the myth is just as important as the reality, after all. Jack the Myth rather than Jack the Ripper.[11]

It is the *man* we must concern ourselves with and not the myth. When we do that, when we throw away all the mystery and self-inspired fantasy, then we *can* get to grips with our Jack the Ripper. Not to say that we can catch him – though it is early days yet in our investigation and who knows by the time we reach the end we may have snapped us our man?

2 35 Dorset Street

There must be somebody there, because somebody must have said 'Nobody'.

Crossingham's Lodging House, 35 Dorset Street is an address full of mystery, coincidence and very likely the solution to the identity of Jack the Ripper.

In any investigation, whether brutal murder is discussed or simple theft, there may well be a certain amount of coincidence present and often it can be quite safely dismissed as that – circumstantial events that inexplicably coincide. But when there are just too many, then any investigator should pause for thought and ask themselves what exactly is going on.

There is no doubt that if the police in many of this century's greatest murder hunts, like the Yorkshire Ripper or Ted Bundy case, had taken the curious coincidences that appeared during their investigations more seriously they would have caught their killers a lot quicker. Coincidence certainly resulted in the execution of the American mass murderer Ted Bundy who tried to explain away the overwhelming circumstantial evidence against him as pure coincidence and amazingly enough the police and the courts went along with him ... to a certain extent. For four long and terrible years Bundy murdered many – the number is not known but is thought to be somewhere between twenty and forty – young girls at his pleasure and without a lot of hindrance from what must have been a remarkably inept police force. The police were already aware that a series of brutal rapes and murders in the Seattle area had been committed by a handsome college type driving a battered brown Volkswagen, in fact even his name was known and the murders were named after him: the 'Ted Murders'. But Ted had moved to Salt Lake City and had begun murdering and raping there as well as in Colorado. Again hordes of witnesses mentioned the brown VW and the college type, and one would have thought that when a policeman arrested the young college type at the wheel of a battered, brown VW for jumping a red light and he gave his name as Ted Bundy some lights would have clicked on in the upstairs of the police department. Especially when a search of Bundy's car revealed that Ted was equipped with handcuffs and panty hose with holes cut out for the eyes. But no, Bundy was released on his own recognizance that same night with the police believing him to be some kind of amateur thief. A very bad piece of police work which was to cost an unknown number of young girls (some believe as many as twenty) their lives – raped and murdered in horrifying circumstances. This could have been avoided had the police acted on the obvious: that when Ted Bundy was in Seattle young girls were raped and murdered by a man named Ted driving a brown VW, that when Ted Bundy was in Salt Lake City young girls were raped and murdered by a man named Ted driving a brown VW, that when Ted Bundy was in Colorado young girls in Colorado were raped and murdered by a man named Ted driving a brown VW. Bundy's ex-girlfriend had even informed the police that he was their man but the officers who subsequently interviewed him couldn't believe that this nice young law student could be the mass murderer they were seeking.

Even more remarkable was the case of Peter Sutcliffe, the 'Yorkshire Ripper', who murdered thirteen women over a period of five years in the north of England in the

1970s. The police effort to catch the killer was massive but Sutcliffe eluded them until quite by chance he was picked up by a routine police patrol in a red-light area because his car carried stolen number plates. Subsequently police records revealed that as early as August 1969 Sucliffe had attacked and beaten a prostitute around the head with a stone wrapped in a sock, and one month later he was caught by police crouched in the garden of a house with a hammer clutched in his hand (many of the murdered women were battered with a hammer). His car had been logged twice by police officers investigting the murders in various red-light areas, his name had been on the police computer as one who frequently picked up prostitutes in the murder area – many of his victims were prostitutes – and like Bundy he had even been interviewed by murder detectives, but just as in the case of Bundy the police were satisfied that Sutcliffe was not their killer.

It is rather frightening to realize that the massive police effort mounted to trap the Yorkshire Ripper totally failed to pick up the six references in their own information systems which would have pointed them directly to Peter Sutcliffe. It would have been possible to explain away two references to the same man as coincidence in the murder enquiry but six references had to mean that Sutcliffe was their man.[1]

Sad to say, though, that even today most murderers tend to be caught by pure luck rather than good police work. In the case of Jack the Ripper there are also far, far too many coincidences, and over a hundred years later it is impossible to believe that, firstly, the police did not react to these startling coincidences at the time. For if they had, they would have surely caught the Ripper, but then as we have seen the modern police forces of the world seem almost as reluctant to react to the information under their control. Secondly, why, when we are discussing one of the most popular literary subjects of our century have legions of writers and researchers not gradually tumbled to these glaringly obvious coincidences that leap out of the pages of their own books?[2]

But back to 1888 and 35 Dorset Street after that slight diversion into the world of modern murder. In 1888 it is thought that there were as many as 233 common lodging houses in the Whitechapel area, and this is quoted to show that Crossingham's Lodging House, 35 Dorset Street, was not the only common lodging house available to the poor and needy of that grim area of London at the time of the murders.[3] The cost of a bed in one of these boarding houses was four pence a night, which was about the same as what one of the more than 1,200 working prostitutes of the area could expect to earn from a 'trick'. Four pence was also what the slaughtermen could earn for each sheep they killed and dressed in the hell that was the nearby underground slaughter yard north of St Paul's where the poor animals were first thrown live into a pit to break their legs before having their throats cut.[4]

Life was 'cheap' in Whitechapel in those days amongst the almost million impoverished inhabitants crammed into a few dirty square miles, and many of the prostitutes were badly mishandled by their clients, beaten up, disfigured and some even had their throats cut. The cry of 'murder!' was so common that it was simply ignored, as was amply demonstrated by a certain Francis Hewitt when giving evidence at the inquest into the murder of Martha Tabram, who some consider to be the first Ripper victim. Martha Tabram was done to death not twelve feet from Mr Hewitt's bedroom window. With his wife he had heard a cry of 'murder!' but explained that: ' … the district around here is rather rough and cries of murder are of frequent, if not a nightly occurrence in the district'.[5] So together they ignored the cry for help and Martha Tabram was brutally murdered.

The mid to late Victorian era was a time of brutal violence. Over 11,000 people died yearly from acts of violence[6] and in what was proudly known as the age of 'assertive masculinity'[7] the poor and needy of London were commonly referred to by their betters as 'surplus population'.[8] Surplus they were indeed when one considers that almost 60 per cent of all children of the area died before they were five,[9] and when one of this surplus population happened to be female she could expect little help from the criminal justice system. In just one sad example a man attacked a girl in broad daylight and beat her so severely that one eye was gouged out and her nose and skull broken. Not satisfied with that he then kicked her as she lay bleeding on the ground and finally threw her over a parapet. For this horrific attack the man was jailed for a mere year. A boy who spun a top on the public highway received the same sentence.[10] Perhaps even more horrific in that age of 'assertive masculinity' was the attack on Jane Shore at a fair in broad daylight by a gang of five men who beat and brutally raped her while a crowd of onlookers cheered them on.[11] Yes, life was cheap but with the advent of Jack the Ripper life was to become cheaper than it was ever before.

Most Ripper authors take their starting point for the murders as Mary Ann Nichols who was killed on Friday 31 August at 3 a.m. in Buck's Row, Whitechapel; and most of these authors are adamant that no other murder before this was the work of the Ripper. This is clearly open to disagreement.

On Tuesday 6 August 1888 at about 5 a.m., PC Barrett was summoned by a John Reeves to examine the mutilated body of a woman he had found lying in a pool of blood on the landing of his lodgings at 37 George Yard Buildings. She had been stabbed thirty-nine times all over her torso, special attention having been paid to the reproductive organs by the killer.

Despite intensive police activity the killer of the prostitute, Martha Tabram (or Turner as she was also known), was never apprehended. Since then the brutal murder has been put down as an isolated case unconnected with the later series of murders attributed to the Ripper. Her death is seen as not matching the 'form' of the Ripper because her throat wasn't cut and she wasn't mutilated in the same fashion as the other victims ... but what was the 'form' of the Ripper?

We only have to look at the case of Long Liz Stride, murdered on the 30 September 1888, where only her throat was cut and no other mutilations whatsoever were carried out. This doesn't match the 'form' of our Ripper either, but no matter the other experts insist that Long Liz was indeed a victim of the Ripper – he was merely disturbed before he could finish the grisly job.

It seems rather naïve to claim Long Liz as a victim of the Ripper because her throat was slit and then to go on and totally dismiss Martha Tabram as a possible victim of the Ripper because she only had been ripped apart by a knife wielding maniac who had inflicted multiple wounds all over her torso, and had attempted by all accounts to cut the reproductive organs out of her body.

No, this was not a simple revenge murder or a vicious disagreement between drunken customer and client, this was the handiwork of a maniac out of control, judging by the number of stab wounds. So how many Jack the Rippers were there running around on the streets of Whitechapel in 1888?

The whole conception of what the 'Ripperologists' are fond of calling the 'form' of Jack the Ripper is fairly spurious anyway. What they seem to claim is that a killer has a method of killing and *never* varies it, a weird sort of 'hallmark' that identifies his work immediately. In other words our 'Ripperologists' are quite prepared to dismiss one or other of the possible victims of Jack the Ripper because the assault was carried out with a different type of weapon, a rounded knife as opposed to a pointed knife and so on. A glaring example of this can be found in Colin Wilson's and Robin Odell's book *Jack the Ripper, summing up and verdict* where the murder and mutilation of Alice

McKenzie aka Claypipe Alice is discussed. Her body was discovered at 1 a.m. on the 17 July 1889 in Castle Alley, Whitechapel, throat stabbed and various cutting and stabbing mutilations to her lower torso. One of the doctors, Thomas Bond, who had previously examined other Ripper victims, called to examine the body and pronounced without hesitation: 'I am of the opinion that the murder was performed by the same person who committed the former series of Whitechapel Murders.'[12]

That is the first-hand testimony of a professional police surgeon with 'hands on' knowledge of the case he is talking about in 1889. One hundred years later our two armchair 'Ripperologists' Odell and Wilson claim that this murder could not possibly have been the Ripper's work because the woman had been stabbed and not cut.[13] This curious obsession with the 'form' of a killer cannot really be defended anyway. After all a 'clever' killer would not have any 'form', and what of the 'form' of other mass murderers?

It is worth briefly mentioning just a few examples now although we will be returning to the subject in a later chapter. The 'Düsseldorf Murderer', Peter Kürten, held the region around the city of Düsseldorf in Germany in absolute terror for almost twenty years, raping, mutilating and murdering so many victims that he himself could give no accurate estimate. He had no 'form', his victims ranged from 10-year-old girls to middle-aged men and he variously strangled them, cut their throats, beat them with a hammer or stabbed them with either scissors, knife or screwdriver. The so-called 'Black-out Ripper', Gordon Cummins, who murdered women during the black-outs in London in 1942 doesn't fit in with our 'Ripperologists' ' idea of a mass murderer either. His first victim was strangled, the second had her throat slit and her stomach mutilated with a tin opener, the third and fourth strangled and mutilated with a razor blade. The 'Yorkshire Ripper' variously employed a screwdriver, hacksaw blade, hammer and knife to murder and mutilate his victims.

If we do dismiss this question of 'form' for the moment then it seems likely that Martha Tabram could after all have been a victim of the Ripper, but whether she was the first will always be open to question, for it is highly unlikely that the Ripper began his terrible career with full-blown murder accompanied by vicious mutilations.

On the night of her murder Martha Tabram had been drinking in the White Swan (some claim the Angel and Crown) with another prostitute, Mary Ann Connelly, and two soldier clients (these were later cleared of any complicity in the murder), and it is Mary Ann Connelly that we must interest ourselves in because her place of residence was Crossingham's Lodging House, 35 Dorset Street.

Mary Ann Connelly was a well-known figure in Whitechapel, better known to her clients and the police as Pearly Poll and she had been associating with Martha Tabram for about six months, but it is not only her address that is interesting. Mary Ann Connelly and two other prostitutes, both also resident at 35 Dorset Street, gave statements in the next two murders ascribed to the Ripper. After the deaths of Mary Ann Nichols and Annie Chapman, all three prostitutes were interviewed by an Inspector Reid and they implicated a man they were all familiar with. It follows that if Mary Ann Connelly and her two friends suspected someone that they knew personally as being the Ripper, then this suspicion must have first been aroused by the murder of Martha Tabram, and later compounded by the murders of Mary Ann Nichols and Annie Chapman. Interestingly enough Walter Dew, the detective who later caught Crippen, noted that Pearly Poll vanished out of the Whitechapel area for days after the murder of her friend, convinced that she would be the next victim.[14]

What is of greater significance is that there is now a link, however slight, between the murders of Martha Tabram, Mary Ann Nichols and Annie Chapman and that link is 35 Dorset Street.

That link becomes even stronger when we investigate

the murder of Annie Chapman the Ripper's next victim, for Dark Annie as she was known actually *lived* at Crossingham's Lodging House, 35 Dorset Street. It is now obvious that we are dealing with a group of prostitutes, all of whom were known to each other and all of whom entertained suspicions about the identity of Jack the Ripper. The random factor – that the killer picked his victims at random and as opportunity presented them – employed by many previous authors starts to slip away as quickly as their all powerful Ripper.[15]

After the murder of Annie Chapman, rumour was rife in Whitechapel that a mysterious individual known as 'Leather Apron' was responsible for the series of murders and the police took up the trail. One of the first clues came from a Timothy Donovan who claimed that he not only knew Leather Apron well but had once turned him out of his lodging house because he had attacked a woman there … and which lodging house was Timothy Donovan the keeper of?

Crossingham's, 35 Dorset Street.

Another resident of 35 Dorset Street, a Mr West, also confirmed that he knew 'Leather Apron' by sight and had observed him hanging around the lodging house in the weeks leading up to the series of murders. Now the coincidences are building up to a point where they cannot be denied or explained away. Remember we are talking about an area of London with over 1,200 working prostitutes and 233 lodging houses, and the laws of chance will simply not explain away the facts that all the prostitutes murdered up till now knew each other and that they were all, in one way or another, connected to 35 Dorset Street. Also, the police acting on evidence from the keeper of that same lodging house soon after arrested a former lodger of that very same lodging house called John Pizer aka 'Leather Apron'. The police eventually let Pizer walk free, even after the man admitted to having hidden himself since the murder of Annie Chapman, was identified by independent witnesses as someone they had seen threatening to knife women, and after discovering a collection of formidable knives at his home. This somewhat strange individual who was known to one and all as 'Jack' was able to provide an alibi for his whereabouts on the nights in question, an alibi with which the police were surprisingly and suspiciously quickly satisfied with.

Now we have the problem of Elizabeth Stride, Long Liz, who is the subject of the next chapter, and the problem rests on whether we are prepared to accept her as the third or fourth victim of Jack the Ripper, or as a victim of Jack the Ripper at all. It is very tempting for this writer to accept that Stride was murdered by the Ripper, as a few days before her death she was actually living at 35 Dorset Street and her boyfriend, Michael Kidney, was living there when she died. If she was a victim of the Ripper then it would truly continue the remarkable coincidences attached to this address and convincingly demonstrate that 35 Dorset Street was linked to the Ripper case. Sadly the temptation has to be avoided, as facts disclosed in the next chapter strongly indicate that Stride was not a Ripper victim.

Catherine Eddowes the fourth, or fifth, victim of the Ripper was found murdered shortly after Long Liz Stride on Sunday 30 September 1888 at 1.45 a.m. in Mitre Square. At first sight there seems to be no link between Catherine Eddowes and 35 Dorset Street, but there are a number of factors concerning her case which do lead us in that general direction: firstly the bloody sink that was discovered by the police in Dorset Street following the trail of the Ripper that night, and secondly the behaviour of Catherine Eddowes on the day before her murder. She had recently returned from hop-picking in Kent with her boyfriend, John Kelly, and not being able to afford a bed in a lodging house took herself off to a casual ward in Shoe Lane where she could get a bed for the night. This was standard practice for the prostitutes of Whitechapel who couldn't find the four pence for a night at a lodging house.

The superintendent of the casual ward told the *East London Observer* on 13 October 1888 that Eddowes had said to him: 'I have come back to earn the reward offered for the apprehension of the Whitechapel murderer. I think I know him.'

This rather astonishing claim has been largely dismissed since then, but it seems rather odd for Catherine Eddowes to have made such a claim on 28 September and then just two days later to fall victim to the Ripper or the Whitechapel murderer as he was then known. A day before her murder she pawned a pair of boots at a shop in Church Street for two shillings and sixpence but curiously gave her name as 'Jane Kelly'. Later in the day she was arrested for drunken behaviour and placed in the cells of Bishopsgate Police Station. On her release, forty-five minutes before she was murdered, she gave her name as 'Mary Ann Kelly' and her address as 6 Fashion Street. How curious it was that literally moments before her deadly encounter with Jack the Ripper she used the *exact* name of the next victim of the Ripper ... Mary Jane Kelly, or as she was fond of calling herself, Mary Ann Kelly. Catherine Eddowes' entire behaviour on the day before her murder was a little bit mysterious, disappearing for most of the day on a supposed mission to visit her daughter and borrow some money as she was broke as was her boyfriend John Kelly. But as her daughter had moved and Eddowes didn't know where she was living this doesn't sound very plausible, and then later turning up in Aldgate so blind drunk – pretending to be a fire engine by all accounts – that she was immediately arrested by a police officer who had difficulty in keeping her standing. Remember she was supposed to have had no money. Her behaviour and her claim that she knew who Jack the Ripper was, plus her use of the next victim's name seems to indicate that Catherine Eddowes did indeed entertain suspicions about the identity of the Ripper and perhaps this is what led to her violent murder. It is worth mentioning in passing that Catherine Eddowes was murdered and mutilated not ten feet from the front door of a police constable living in Mitre Square and, as already stated, just forty-five minutes after being released from the custody of the police.

The last murder attributed to the Ripper, that of Mary Jane Kelly on Friday 9 November 1888 between 3.30 a.m. and 4 p.m. at 13 Miller's Court, well and truly continues the amazing string of coincidences. For 13 Miller's Court was in fact part of 26/27 Dorset Street and the building directly across the street was none other than Crossingham's, 35 Dorset Street. On the evening of her death Mary Jane Kelly had spent some of the time in the company of Lizzie Albrook who worked at an unspecified lodging house in Dorset Street, and, before moving into Miller's Court, Kelly had lived at Paternoster Row in Dorset Street where another suspect, Joseph Isaacs, in the Ripper murders had also lived.

On the night of Mary Jane Kelly's murder Sarah Lewis, who was returning to her 'doss' in Miller's Court at 2.30 p.m. saw a man leaning against the wall of 35 Dorset Street staring across the road at the entrance to Miller's Court. The trail keeps coming back to 35 Dorset Street. An even later murder of a prostitute, Frances Coles, in 1891, that the 'Ripperologists' dismiss as the work of the Ripper, is also of interest as she too lived at 35 Dorset Street.

Why have all the 'Ripperologists' up till now totally ignored the relevance of 35 Dorset Street when it is so obvious that 35 Dorset Street is a vital clue to the identity of Jack the Ripper? One can, with a little sympathy, understand the reluctance of the police in 1888 to carry out intensive investigations into any activity connected with Dorset Street as the street was considered to be one of the most dangerous in the whole of London. The police were likely to be set upon by the local roughs and toughs and savagely beaten, unless they went in with a considerable force of men. But the 'Ripperologists' sat safely in their armchairs a hundred years later do not have the same excuse. Colin Wilson and others have said in their books that the Ripper was probably a very ordinary man and have then gone on to largely ignore this very ordinary man. They fail even to present vital background material on such important ordinary men as Michael Kidney, Elizabeth 'Long Liz' Stride's boyfriend, a man known for his violent behaviour, or Timothy Donovan, keeper of Crossingham's Lodging House who appeared regularly in court during 1888 charged with violent assaults and eventually murdered his wife in 1904. Instead they have presented elaborate chapters where, variously, dukes, distinguished doctors, black magicians, Russian secret agents, poets and painters are all tramped before us as likely candidates for the role of the Ripper. Ignoring their ordinary man they instead devote several chapters to outlining the hideous mutilations inflicted on the Ripper's victims, and the supposed psychology behind these mutilations and murders which have been described by Colin Wilson as the first sex murders as we know them. But where is their ordinary man, and were the crimes of Jack the Ripper really sex murders?

3 Long Liz

Do you think it's a-a-a- Woozle?

Elizabeth Stride (aka Long Liz) was murdered on 30 September 1888 between 12.30 p.m. and 1.00 p.m. at 40 Berner Street, Whitechapel, and it is claimed by almost all writing on the subject of the murders that she was the third victim of Jack the Ripper. The fact that only Long Liz's throat was cut and there was no other mutilations or signs of violence on her body are claimed as proof that the Ripper was disturbed at his work and was unable to finish the destructive task to his strange satisfaction. This is very likely a false assumption. From the available evidence it seems clear that Long Liz was not a victim of Jack the Ripper, rather she was perhaps the victim of a domestic quarrel which sadly ended in a vicious act of violence. In the climate of hysteria generated by the first two attacks (or three, depending whether Martha Tabram was a victim of the Ripper) where the women were badly mutilated it was easy to see this as another, albeit failed, strike by the Ripper. It was also easy for the man who actually cut Long Liz's throat to use this as a cover to escape suspicion.

To begin with Long Liz does not really fit the profile of the other women attacked by Jack the Ripper, who were all working prostitutes, well known in the Whitechapel area and well known to the police. There is no doubt that Long Liz did resort to prostitution, but it seems to have only been when she had no other choice, preferring to earn her money in other ways as attested to by several witnesses. The lodging house deputy, Elizabeth Tanner, at 32 Flower and Dean Street where Long Liz was staying at the time of her death described her as a 'very quiet woman who ... did cleaning work for the Jews'. The bedmaker at the same lodging house, Ann Mill, pointed out that: 'Stride worked when she could get work and a better hearted, more good natured, cleaner woman never lived.'[1]

Thomas Bates the watchman at 32 Flower and Dean Street also testified that Long Liz tried to make her living 'charring'. Add to this the fact that she often called at the Swedish Church to apply for financial aid, and received it several times – Long Liz was Swedish in origin – and that to earn money she would also clean the rooms of the lodging houses where she stayed.[2] Somehow this behaviour just doesn't fit in with the profile and activities of a habitual prostitute who earned money by the simple act of selling her body for four pence a time and then went straight to the nearest drinking house and drank herself insensible. No, the behaviour and activities of Long Liz shortly before her murder lead one rather to the conclusion that here was a woman who cared about her appearance, was determined to do anything else to earn a living rather than reducing herself to prostitution, like cleaning rooms and begging aid from churches, and that she had some kind of future planned for herself.

We must now examine the events of the night leading up to Long Liz's murder. Long Liz's boyfriend, Michael Kidney, claimed that the last time he had seen her was on 25 September when she left their shared room at 35 Dorset Street and that he fully expected to find her at home when he returned from work that evening. However at the inquest a woman called Catherine Lane, who had known Long Liz for six or seven years, claimed that Long Liz had told her that she had in fact left Kidney after a row. Kidney strongly denied this at the inquest. But the fact that he admitted that Long Liz had left him before, on several occasions, would seem to indicate that theirs was a stormy relationship at best. He estimated that out of the three years they had been living together, she had lived apart from him for at least five months in total. The fact that he was always willing to take her back means that either he was in love with her, or he was financially dependent on her. As he was working at the time of her murder, as a waterside labourer, it is probably safer to assume that he was in love with her. Unlike most of the other Ripper victims, Long Liz, an unusually tall woman of Swedish origins, appears from her photograph to have been a reasonably attractive woman. Detective Walter Dew noted that she had an unusual prettiness and other writers have since commented on her attractiveness.[3]

Also, it has to be asked, if they had not had a row why then would Long Liz have moved out of Kidney's room at 35 Dorset Street and taken up lodgings at 32 Flower and Dean Street? The circumstances strongly indicate that Long Liz had made up her mind to leave Kidney once again, and it was obviously not for the reason of being able to pursue a trouble-free life as a prostitute, otherwise she would not have spent the entire day cleaning rooms at the lodging house to earn sixpence on the day of her death. A Whitechapel prostitute in 1888 charged her customers four pence, a sum that could be earned in the space of a few minutes, therefore it seems highly unlikely that a habitual prostitute would spend her entire day cleaning rooms for a mere sixpence when she was expecting to ply her trade that same evening.

On the night of her murder Long Liz briefly visited the Queen's Head public house in Commercial Road at around 6.30 p.m., and then was back at the lodging house at Flower and Dean Street between 7 p.m. and 8 p.m., preparing to go out for the evening. The watchman at the lodging house, Thomas Bates, described her manner as 'cheerful', and as she went to the trouble of borrowing a clothes brush from another lodger, Charles Preston, it was obvious that she was keen to appear at her best for someone. She also gave another lodger, Catherine Lane, a piece of velvet to look after and this may well have been a gift she had received earlier in the evening. At any event the fact that she had a 'date' seems obvious, and this date was certainly not with Michael Kidney as he gave evidence at the inquest that he did not see Long Liz again after she left him on 25 September. After Long Liz left the lodging house she was not seen again until just before 11 p.m. by two men, J. Best and John Gardner, coming out of the Bricklayer's Arms, Settles Street, with a man. Mr Best's statement was as follows:

> They had been served in the public house, and went out when me and my friends came in. It was raining very fast and they did not appear willing to go out. He was hugging and kissing her, and as he seemed a respectably dressed man, we were rather astonished at the way he was going on with the woman.

And after admitting that he and his friends barracked the man he said ' ... he and the woman went off like a shot soon after eleven.'[4] After this another witness, Matthew Packer, said that he had sold a bunch of grapes to Long Liz and her male companion in Berner Street sometime between 11 p.m. and midnight. Most writers on the subject of the Ripper are inclined to dismiss Packer's statement on the grounds that he was an unreliable witness. But there are other factors which back his statement up. Not least that his testimony was felt to be so important that it was personally taken down by Sir Charles Warren, the Metropolitan Police Commissioner at the time of the murders. Also the discoverer of Long Liz's body, Louis Deimschutz, told the *Evening News* that she *did* indeed have a bunch of grapes clutched in one hand, and at the inquest Dr Phillips who performed the post-mortem said that there were fruit stains on the handkerchiefs he had found on the body. Two other witnesses, Mrs Rosenfield and Eva Hartstein, who lived in the passage on Berner Street where Long Liz was murdered also claimed to have seen a blood-soaked grape stalk and red and white flower petals before the police washed the blood away. Later a detective, searching the drain in the yard, did discover a grape stalk.

Many authors view the inquest evidence of Dr Phillips as conclusive proof of Packer's unreliability as a witness, for the doctor found no sign of grape skins or pips in the stomach of the murdered woman. It is of course quite possible to buy a bunch of grapes without actually eating them. However it is important to note that Long Liz's teeth were found to be in an appalling state at the post mortem with all the teeth from the lower left jaw missing. Detectives searching the murder area subsequently found several spat-out grape skins and seeds, and this could very well be the reason why Dr Phillips was unable to identify the fruit in her stomach, as the crushed pulp of the grape flesh would have been easily overlooked, if not impossible to identify.

So Packer's statement cannot be dismissed lightly, and it is an important statement, not just because it identifies the whereabouts of the murder victim at a given time, but because it poses an equally important question. If Long Liz was a common prostitute and the man seen with her was merely one of the night's many 'pick-ups' why was he buying her grapes? A man who casually picks up a prostitute in a pub, does not normally treat her to anything other than the cost of her bodily favours. He doesn't usually buy her flowers to pin on her coat either, but it appears that this man did just that. PC William Smith, whose beat was Berner Street, saw Long Liz and her male companion at 12.30 p.m. and testified that she was wearing a red flower pinned to her jacket. Remember the flower petals discovered by the two women in Berner's Passage.

The care that Long Liz seemed to have put into her

appearance on that night, her cheerful attitude as attested to by her fellow lodgers, and the earlier statement from Mr Best about the actions of the couple he encountered leaving the Bricklayer's Arms does not sound much like a prostitute and a 'pick-up'. They come across like lovers, perhaps secret lovers but lovers all the same. When her body was discovered she was still clutching a small packet of 'cachous' – not 'cashew nuts' as some Ripperologists maintain – in her left hand. Cachous are small French pastilles designed to sweeten the breath of smokers and are still very popular today. This is another indication of her intention to be at her best for someone that evening. After all if we are to believe Donald Rumblelow's account of the sexual activities of Victorian prostitutes it is obvious that sweet breath was not an essential requirement.

Remember, PC William Smith saw them both in Berner Street at 12.30 p.m. and they had left the nearby pub 'soon after eleven', and they were possibly seen kissing in Berner Street by William Marshall, a labourer, at 11.45 p.m. Therefore this was no quick and business-like liaison between prostitute and client for four pence. It would appear to be the actions of a couple who know they have to part but are stretching out their time together for as long as possible. This would seem to indicate that the man with Long Liz was a married man with a wife waiting at home for him, otherwise the two could have easily spent the night together.

The next sighting of Long Liz at 12.45 p.m. is of great importance. A Hungarian named Israel Schwartz did not give evidence at the inquest of Long Liz, but he did make a statement to the police. This statement remained unpublished until very recently when the Home Office files were made available:

> Israel Schwartz of 22 Helen Street, Backchurch Lane, stated that at this hour, on turning into Berner Street from Commercial Street, and having got as far as the gateway

> where the murder was committed, he saw a man stop and speak to a woman, who was standing in the gateway. The man tried to pull the woman into the street, but he turned her round and threw her down on the footway and the woman screamed three times, but not very loudly. On crossing to the opposite side of the street, he saw a second man standing lighting his pipe. The man who threw the woman down called out, apparently to the man on the opposite side of the road, 'Lipski', and then Schwartz walked away, but finding that he was followed by the second man, he ran as far as the railway arch, but the man did not follow so far.
>
> Schwartz cannot say whether the two men were together or known to each other. Upon being taken to the mortuary Schwartz identified the body as that of the woman he had seen ...[5]

Inspector Abberline, who was involved with investigations into all the Ripper murders added:

> I questioned Israel Schwartz very closely at the time he made the statement as to whom the man addressed when he called Lipski, but he was unable to say. Also it was never ascertained whether the man lighting his pipe ran after Schwartz or ran because he, too, was alarmed by the man who had thrown the woman to the ground.[6]

This strange encounter took place just fifteen minutes before the body of Long Liz was discovered by Louis Diemschutz as he attempted to bring his pony and cart into the yard of the Berner Street Club at 1.00 a.m. Therefore it seems obvious that the man Schwartz saw throwing Long Liz to the ground was her murderer. It would seem highly unlikely that this was the same man who had earlier been with her in the pub 'kissing and cuddling' blatantly in front of a group of men, dallying with her in the street in front of numerous witnesses including a patrolling policeman, and not an hour before affectionately buying her fruit and flowers. Rather this would have been the man Schwartz saw on the other side of the street, observing the scene from a discreet distance while smoking his pipe.

It is necessary to look at the descriptions of these two men. Schwartz described the man he saw assaulting Long Liz: ' … about 30, 5ft 5ins., with a fair complexion, dark hair, small brown moustache, full face and broad shoulders. He was wearing a dark jacket and trousers, and a black cap with a peak.' The man on the opposite side of the street he described as: ' … 35, 5ft 11ins., with fresh complexion, light brown hair and brown moustache. He was dressed in a dark overcoat and an old black hard felt hat with a wide brim.' The man that PC William Smith saw earlier, at 12.30 a.m. with Long Liz he described as: 'The man was aged about 28, was 5ft 7ins. in height, of dark complexion and sporting a small dark moustache. He was wearing a black diagonal coat, hard felt hat, white collar and tie.' Therefore it would seem that the man PC William Smith encountered walking with Long Liz at 12.30 p.m. was the same man Israel Schwartz saw watching the attack on Long Liz, from the other side of Berner Street at 12.45 p.m. The hard felt hat clinches it. The man assaulting Long Liz was wearing a cap with a peak.

The man with the peaked cap may have been dogging the movements of Liz Stride and her 'gentleman' since they left the Bricklayer's Arms, or he may have come across them in Berner Street quite by chance. Whatever, the description of this man would seem to indicate that he was of the 'working class' rather than a 'gentleman', the peaked cap as opposed to a hard felt hat. Long Liz and her companion must have become aware that they were being followed, and she probably knew exactly who it was that was following them. Otherwise, why would her companion have left her standing in the gateway of 40 Berner Street and crossed the road to await events at a discreet distance? When Long Liz realized they were being followed and that the man following them was someone with a grudge against her and her new companion, it would have been natural for her to have advised her 'gentleman' to cross the road while she sorted the situation out. In Schwartz's evidence he said that: ' ... he saw a man stop and speak to a woman, who was standing in the gateway. The man tried to pull the woman into the street, but he turned her round and threw her down on the footway and the woman screamed three times, but not very loudly.'

If the man in the peaked cap had been a robber or murderer he would not have attempted to pull Long Liz *out* of the passageway into the street, he would have tried to push her back *into* the darkness of the passageway. If the man in the peaked cap had been a robber or murderer unknown to Long Liz she would have screamed her head off when attacked. Remember that two women had already been brutally murdered on the streets of Whitechapel and if the attacker had really been unknown to her she would certainly have protested with a lot more vigour than is apparent from Schwartz's description. No, this scene has more of the feel of a domestic dispute about it, rather than the cold-blooded calculated actions of a vicious murderer about to disembowel his victim.

What was it that this attacker called out to the man on the opposite side of the street according to Schwartz? 'Lipski.' This was an insult specifically used against Jews after a Jew called Lipski murdered a woman in 1887. Earlier we have seen that the landlady, Elizabeth Tanner, at 32 Flower and Dean Street had said of Long Liz that she was 'a very quiet woman who sometimes stayed out late at night and did cleaning work for the Jews'. It is possible that Long Liz, during her spells of cleaning work for the Jews, may have met a man with whom she struck up a relationship (of course she may also have met a man casually in a pub or elsewhere). It may have been this relationship which had soured her on-off co-habitation and friendship with Michael Kidney, leading to the eventual row – as testified to by Catherine Lane – that led to Long Liz eventually moving out of their shared Dorset Street room. This would seem to be confirmed by Michael Kidney when he told the inquest into her death that Long Liz was fluent in Yiddish, a strange accomplishment indeed for a woman of Swedish origins.

In terms of human relationships, times have not much changed since 1888 and if Long Liz was forced to separate from Michael Kidney on numerous occasions it was probably because he used violence against her. Even today many women are prepared to suffer a certain degree of mental and physical abuse to hold a relationship together, but there is only one answer to violence and that is to walk out of the door. That Long Liz's and Michael Kidney's relationship was not quite as rosy as he painted it is obvious from his inquest testimony when he admitted that he always padlocked the door to his and Stride's (Long Liz) room at Crossingham's Lodging House, 35 Dorset Street, and that he had the only key. This is the act of a domineering individual, one used to his own way, rather than a man prepared to share and share alike. It is not normal behaviour in a relationship to lock one's female partner out of the house for the whole day while one is at work. One must also compare this statement to his other inquest testimony where he said that he fully expected to find Long Liz back at home in Dorset Street on 25 September. How? She didn't have a key.

The fact of the matter is that Kidney was a violent man, a drunkard and a brawler, who was sent down by a court for his unruly behaviour in July 1888, and had assaulted Long Liz in the past. She even went to the extent of having him arrested on one occasion in 1887, but when he was charged in court she failed to appear against him and the case was dismissed. It is likely that she feared the punishment of Kidney more than he feared the punishment of the court.

The behaviour of the gentleman who was with Long Liz

on the night of the murder is another indication that he was possibly married and 'respectable'. He stood on the opposite side of the road smoking his pipe and then making off quickly when the man in the peaked cap began his assault. He didn't want to get involved, it would have meant a lot of awkward questions and he had after all come out for an evening of fun and wasn't about to mix it with a ruffian of the nature that was attacking his mistress. Any other man would have enlisted the aid of Schwartz as he approached and then frightened off Long Liz's attacker. But no, this 'gentleman', like Schwartz, decided discretion was the better part of valour and in consequence Long Liz was brutally murdered.

The suspicion for this brutal murder must fall on Michael Kidney. His denial at the inquest that he had rowed with Long Liz shortly before her murder is highly suspicious, as Catherine Lane who swore at the inquest that Kidney had fallen out with Long Liz had no reason whatsoever to lie. She had, remember, known Long Liz for almost seven years and had nothing to gain by lying after her death. Rows in a relationship are not an uncommon thing and for Kidney to deny this can only be explained by an ulterior motive and that motive was to cover his guilt. It was he who had followed Long Liz and her new friend, it must have been, otherwise she would not have sent her man across the street while she dealt with Kidney. After all, she had lived with Kidney for three years and probably felt she was capable of calming him down. When the attacker threw her to the ground she did not scream out at the top of her voice 'murder!' as would have been normal in the situation and in an area where two women had recently been brutally hacked to pieces by a knife-wielding maniac. No, Long Liz knew the man who stood above her on that fateful night and may have expected a thrashing. But, instead, Michael Kidney, after insulting her new Jewish 'gentleman' and then having the satisfaction of seeing him quickly depart, held her down and slit her throat in a fit of rage and jealousy. Then he quickly made his way back to his lodgings, pausing to wash his bloody hands in a public sink actually in Dorset Street, as attested to by police officers searching the area. Then he walked into number 35, home and dry after committing what has been until now the perfect murder.

The final evidence for Michael Kidney's guilt is so surprisingly obvious that it is difficult to believe that it has lain around for so many years without anyone realizing its importance. One day after the murder of Elizabeth Stride (on 1 October 1888) Michael Kidney arrived in a drunken condition at Leman Street Police Station, Whitechapel. He demanded to speak to a detective and ranting and raving that if he had been the constable in the area where the murder took place he would have killed himself.[7]

This is a vital point because Kidney did this before the inquest opened on Elizabeth Stride and her body had still not been identified. Even later, after the inquest had opened, she was still wrongly identified as Elizabeth Stokes. So how then did Kidney know that the latest murder victim was his ex-girlfriend Elizabeth Stride before she had even been identified?[8] Remember he had not seen her for almost a week and later admitted to the inquest jury that he was not 'worried' by her absence. He was also later pressed by the inquest jury to explain why he had gone to Leman Police Station to complain about the police and he came out with a wild tale about having some information which could have trapped the murderer if he had been given control of a group of detectives. When pressed even further he admitted that the tale was a lie.

The truth of the matter is that he did have some information which would have trapped the murderer because he murdered Elizabeth Stride himself. In the classic manner – that will be presented in a later chapter – he presented himself to the police the very next day, in the role of the outraged upright citizen full of complaints about police inefficiency. There is no doubt now that

Kidney did murder Elizabeth Stride … going to the police to complain about the circumstances of her death before anyone knew she was dead clinches it.

It is astonishing that the inquest jury were so quickly satisfied with his testimony, particularly after he admitted lying to them. Equally, one can only wonder at the total incompetence of the police in failing to realize that Kidney could not have known that it was Elizabeth Stride who was murdered before her body had been identified, unless he had committed the crime himself. Again, as in other inquests on the so called 'Ripper' murders, the attitude of the police is quite unbelievable. The failure of the police in Stride's case of not calling the single eyewitness to her murder, Israel Schwartz, to give evidence at the inquest is absolute criminal neglect. For there is no doubt that if Israel Schwartz had been called to the inquest he would have immediately identified Michael Kidney as the man he saw attacking Elizabeth Stride that night in Berner Street.

But was Michael Kidney Jack the Ripper? He is a very tempting suspect, the perfect suspect in many ways. His address, Crossingham's Lodging House, 35 Dorset Street, means that he must have known the group of murdered prostitutes that were all in one way or another connected to this address. We know he was a violent man but now we also know he was a murderer. Criteria that we establish later in the book to profile killers fit Michael Kidney like a glove: he was known to the police as a drunken brawler, he was questioned by police in connection with the murders, he did go to the police voluntarily and make a nuisance of himself, and he must have known the victims personally which would explain the vicious mutilations to the faces of his victims. If he was the Ripper then his territory was so squeezed by police activity that he did eventually murder on his front doorstep – remember Mary Jane Kelly was murdered right opposite 35 Dorset Street. The 'something' which placed him above suspicion in the minds of the prostitutes he murdered could have been his relationship with Liz Stride and the prostitutes of 35 Dorset Street ... he was after all almost family. A perfect candidate for Jack the Ripper? But something is wrong. And that something is Kidney's relationship to Elizabeth Stride, and Kidney himself. Would the Ripper really have killed someone who shared a room with him a week before and also in front of witnesses?

All of the Ripper murders, except that of Stride, show an unmistakable pattern: the victim lured to a dark and lonely spot as if by appointment rather than chance (the murder of Kelly falling out of place perhaps because of the intensive police activity by this time) and then murdered and mutilated with incredible swiftness and savagery. Three witnesses saw another victim, Catherine Eddowes, alive at 1.35 a.m. and only ten minutes later at 1.45 a.m. a police constable discovered her savagely mutilated corpse. If Michael Kidney had been Jack the Ripper he would have had ample time to inflict similar mutilations on Elizabeth Stride, because there was a clear quarter of an hour between the time she was attacked and the discovery of her body. No, it seems perhaps that even Michael Kidney didn't realize he would murder Stride that night and the whole account of their encounter in Berner Street just doesn't read like any of the other cases which may have involved the Ripper.

It will be necessary to take another look at Kidney's character and behaviour in a later chapter and this too will strongly indicate that he wasn't Jack the Ripper. The Ripper story is a complex one and it is essential to explore every avenue that is open to us in an attempt to arrive at the truth of the matter. Earlier we mentioned Colin Wilson's description of the Ripper crimes as being the 'first sex murders of a sexual nature' and it is to this statement that we must now turn our attention.

4 Motives in the Dark

I have just been thinking, and I have come to a very important decision. These are the wrong sort of bees.

Colin Wilson's assertion that the Ripper murders were the first murders of a sexual nature which could be placed in the same category as sex murders of today[1] is an assertion that cannot be left unchallenged because the fact of the matter is that we do not know what motive lay behind the Ripper murders.

It is grasping at thin air to declare that they were 'sex crimes'. It is a simple explanation, too simple perhaps. Must we always assume, as Wilson and countless other writers on the subject do, that when a woman is murdered and mutilated that the killer's motive was sexual gratification, even when there is not a shred of evidence to indicate that any sort of sexual contact took place? Of course, Colin Wilson is prepared to argue this point and he does so at considerable length in various different volumes and his complex theories are very neat and persuasive. For instance, to explain the activities of Peter Sutcliffe, the 'Yorkshire Ripper' – who we have already mentioned in a previous chapter – Wilson links Sutcliffe's inability to achieve an erection or penetration to his subsequent murder and mutilation of the women. What Wilson maintains is that the ritualized stabbing became an obsession which allowed Sutcliffe to achieve orgasm. In other words, the Yorkshire Ripper was raping the women with a knife as a sexual thrill. Of vital importance to note here is that Wilson is basing his explanation on his, Wilson's, own opinion and not the hard facts.[2] The facts seem to indicate that Sutcliffe had no sexual ambitions towards his victims. On the contrary, his behaviour seemed to have been driven by anti-sexual resentment at the activities of women who offered their bodies for money. It should also not be forgotten that Sutcliffe murdered most of his victims with a hammer by striking them across the back of the skull and it is impossible to equate this violent behaviour with a desire for penetration or to commit rape with a knife. There is absolutely no evidence to substantiate the claim that the Yorkshire Ripper experienced any sort of 'sexual thrill' from brutalizing his victims.[3]

Wilson goes on to relate Sutcliffe's and a number of other murderers' motives – like Robert Hansen the Alaskan businessman who hunted twenty prostitutes down with his rifle and shot them or Joachim Kroll who killed, raped and ate his teenage victims – to that of Jack the Ripper's. He claims that in the Ripper type of killer, a feeling of inferiority is determined by the nature of the sexual impulse. According to Wilson those sex killers are typified by their twisted egos.[4] But he is on very dangerous ground here. Hansen the killer-businessman *did* have sex with his victims first and Kroll raped his victims when they were dead. Sutcliffe had no sexual contact with his victims and neither did Jack the Ripper. This is of enormous import and if Wilson had kept his comparison of the Ripper only to Sutcliffe, one could at least understand it from the point of view that neither of the men had sexual contact with their victims. But to make a comparison between a murderer like Hansen who was more than capable of sexual relations with the prostitute he was about to murder – and in fact often let the woman go free unharmed if she satisfied him – and a murderer like Sutcliffe who went out with the idea of actually murdering a prostitute without any forethought of sexual contact is an obvious error. The point being that Hansen viewed his victims as sex objects first and only secondly as murder objects when they failed to satisfy him sexually. Equally the German murderer Kroll viewed his victims as sexual objects but admitted that he was not able, due to a peculiar shyness, to have sexual relations with them while they were still alive, so he murdered them and then abused their corpses. Sutcliffe however seems to have had no intention whatsoever of having sex with his victims, they were to be brutally murdered full stop. Sutcliffe's testimony concerning the murder of his thirteenth victim, Helen Rytka, makes that absolutely clear. His confession was read out to the court: 'She undid my trousers and seemed prepared to start sexual intercourse right away in the front seat of the car. It was very awkward for me to find a way to get her out of the car.' One can detect a note of panic here. He didn't want sex. He wanted to kill her. Finally he got her out of the car by suggesting that they had sex in the back seat and then he attacked her with the hammer but only struck her a glancing blow. Two taxi-drivers almost saw him so he pulled the woman to the ground and:

> I jumped on top of her and covered her mouth with my hand. It seemed like an eternity and she was still struggling. I told her that if she kept quiet she would be all right. As she had got me aroused a moment previous, I had no alternative but to go ahead with the act of sex as the only means of keeping her quiet. It didn't take long. She kept staring at me. She didn't put much into it.

As soon as the taxi-drivers left he brutally murdered her. It is obvious that sex with the woman was the last thing on his mind. He wanted to kill her and if the taxi-drivers had not disturbed him he would have done so without any sort of sexual contact. He was forced to have sex with the woman to keep her quiet. One can only stare into a kind of wasteland of oblivion when considering his comment that the woman he had just beaten over the head with a hammer 'didn't put much into' the act of sex. But what is plainly obvious is that we are talking about two very different breeds of animal here. One kills for sex, the other kills for something else ... but what?

Even more dangerous, perhaps, is Wilson's classification of the famous Bobby Franks murder case as a sexual crime. This took place in the 1920s in America where two wealthy, bored male students kidnapped and murdered a 14-year-old boy, Bobby Franks, to prove that they could get away with the 'perfect murder'. It is difficult to understand why Wilson should classify this as a sex crime when there was absolutely no signs of sexual interference but we are told that the chisel used to kill the boy was a symbolic penis and the culvert into which the body had been thrust a symbolic vagina. Wilson admits that his interpretation, based on Freudian reasoning, is simplistic, but he believes it does show that the murder had a sexual motive and demonstrates that such crimes are by their very nature 'baffling and paradoxical'.[5]

But Wilson's Freudian explanation also illustrates the contradictory nature of our Ripperologists who seem prepared to mislead us, either with their fantastic suspects or complicted theories about the nature of the crimes of Jack the Ripper. There is anyway something quite bizzarre about using Freudian interpretation today. One shouldn't forget that Freud maintained that adult women who stimulated their clitoris to achieve orgasm were being 'childish'. The Hite report on female sexuality demonstrates conclusively that at least 70 per cent of all women *need* to stimulate their clitoris to achieve orgasm.[6]

But to get back to Wilson and his theories. It is well worth examining some of his other statements when it comes to murder and sex. For instance where he ponders over the plight of female murder victims he cites the case of Blanche Fisher who was beaten and murdered in Vancouver in 1949, and wonders why such an attractive woman had remained unmarried.[7] It is almost as though Blanche Fisher had invited murder by being attractive and unmarried. Is Wilson implying that such a woman has no right to enjoy a healthy sex life? But there is worse to come when Wilson discusses sexual crimes against children, maintaining that we are generally disposed to believe that children are the innocent victims of 'lust-crazed maniacs'. He points out that it is, in fact, often the child that instigates sexual activity with the adult.[8] Yes, Colin Wilson is quite right, children do often initiate harmless sexual games, but it is most certainly adults who turn these harmless sexual games into reality and sometimes murder. An innocent child's quest for the facts of life, however, can never be offered as an excuse for rape or murder.

Equally bizzare, perhaps, is Wilson's thinking on the case of the 22-year-old woman who accepted a lift from two men in Kingsport, Tennessee in 1970. They drove her to a nearby quarry and raped her. During the night she was cut and stabbed with a knife and threatened with murder and the next day was raped and beaten consistently. The next night she had to go through the same ordeal again, being eventually released the following day when she promised not to go to the police. She did go to the police and the men were quite rightly jailed for what were pretty horrific crimes. Wilson does admit that the girl was attacked by two sadists but also claims that she was equally to blame.[9] If the reader is perplexed by that assertion, the implication being presumably that women should not accept lifts (although it is important to note here that the girl *did* know the men) Wilson goes on to claim that a female who makes a habit of wearing low-cut dresses can be to blame if she is murdered.[10] Why? Surely a normal masculine reaction to a well-displayed pair of female breasts is pleasure and not murder. Does Wilson really feel that the murder rate goes up and down depending on the year's fashion of cleavage exposure. Do mini-skirts incite murder? If his theory is correct then surely we must find that the murder rate at naturist clubs is significantly higher than at golf clubs?

It is almost as if Colin Wilson is putting his influence towards excusing the mass murderers he is writing about. The victims have invited murder, either by wearing low-cut dresses, accepting lifts off strangers or being a pretty, unmarried woman or even a child who seeks an explanation of the facts of life. Perhaps even more alarming is the behaviour of some obviously disturbed people who appear to have read some of Wilson's work. One famous example was William Macdonald, a homosexual mutilator who savagely murdered and hacked to pieces men he picked up around Sydney, Australia. Police on his trail discovered a copy of Wilson's novel *Ritual in the Dark* wrapped in a bloodstained pillow in Macdonald's house. This story from Wilson concerns the activities of a homosexual mass murderer. Later when police arrested him in Melbourne they found a copy of Colin Wilson's *An Encyclopedia of Murder* in his possession and asked him why he wanted to read such a book. His reply was: 'It's the only thing I get any pleasure from.'[11]

Reading Wilson's considerable output of material related to murder and sex can prove to be a disturbing business. One has to question much of what he says and there are some very 'grey' areas of his speculation indeed. To take just one other casual statement from him where he claims that the root of the male sex drive is aggression, a desire to be the master.[12] On the contrary, many men admire aggressive and strong qualities in women and on a physical level view the act of sex in terms of pleasure seeking rather than aggressive behaviour. The 'Hite Report on Male Sexuality'[13] makes that quite clear, and it also shows that the majority of men see sex on an emotional/psychological level as supplying them with the feeling of being loved and accepted. Many describe sexual intercourse as the ultimate act of acceptance, and some enjoyed sex as an act of pleasurable domination by their female partner. It is clear in this important report on male sexuality that men see sex as an expression of masculinity rather than an act of aggression, only a very small group of males view sex as being aggressive, dominant or conquering and many of these recognized the futility of their behaviour and sought to modify it. What might also surprise Wilson is that 35 per cent of men enjoy being the submissive partner in sex.

Hite's conclusions are of enormous import to the subject which Wilson so casually deals with and Wilson would do well to study his subject before making such facile comments. Hite concluded that the act of sex was one of the only times when a man could drop his masculine, aggressive and dominant role and react in an affectionate manner to the female partner. If Wilson had restricted his comment to the activities of criminal rapists then he might be right but to classify all male sexual behaviour as having its origins in aggression is terribly wrong.

To get back to Jack the Ripper, there are two other points about Wilson's psychological portrait of Jack the Ripper that must be challenged as well. This is not intended as a campaign against Colin Wilson but it must be stressed that he is seen as the 'clearing house' for Ripper theories and his opinion and theories generally carry enormous respect.[14] Where he goes others tend to follow and this is why he must be challenged. Wilson claims that it wasn't until about halfway into the nineteenth century that sex crimes first reared its ugly head, maintaining that the majority of murders up till then had been economic in nature.[15] This is why he views Jack the Ripper as the herald of a new age of 'sex crimes'. Clearly this is a mistaken view when there is strong evidence indicating that cases of criminal sexuality have been known since man first started recording his history, for instance as early as 1200 BC.

Equally startling is Wilson's claim that the rise of pornography dates from the 1820s. What about the *Karma Sutra*? Or the famous illustrations from the reign of Rameses XI – 1153–1070 BC – showing the king indulging his harem in a variety of sexual adventures? No, pornography has been with us probably just as long as the written word.

But back to his contention that most murders were economic until halfway through the nineteenth century. Two cases of brutal rape and murder are graphically documented in the Old Testament. The first from Judges 19:22–30. A wandering Levite and his concubine seek to stay overnight in the city of Gibeah and are taken in by an old man who gives them supper. From the Bible:[16]

> While they were enjoying themselves, some of the wicked men of the city surrounded the house. Pounding on the door, they shouted to the old man who owned the house, 'Bring out the man who came to your house so we can have sex with him.' The owner of the house went outside and said to them, 'No, my friends, don't be so vile. Since this man is my guest, don't do this disgraceful thing. Look, here is my virgin daughter, and his concubine. I will bring them out to you now, and you can use them and do to them whatever you wish. But to this man, don't do such a disgraceful thing.' But the men would not listen to him. So the man took his concubine and sent her outside to them, and they raped her and abused her throughout the night, and at dawn they let her go. At daybreak the woman went back to the house where her master was staying, fell down at the door and lay there until daylight. When her master got up in the morning and opened the door of the house and stepped out to continue on his way, there lay his concubine, fallen in the doorway of the house, with her hands on the threshold. He said to her, 'Get up; let's go.' But there was no answer. Then the man put her on his donkey and set out for home. When he reached home, he took a knife and cut up his concubine, limb by limb, into twelve parts and sent them into all the areas of Israel.

An unpleasant tale, perhaps more so because of the attitude of the Biblical men to their women rather than anything else, but it does contain all the ingredients of a 'real' sex crime much as we might read in one of today's newspapers: threatened homosexual rape, aggressive gang rape and the vicious murder of a helpless woman plus rather perversely the later mutilation of that dead woman.

The next example involves the planned rape of a sister by her brother and cromes from Samuel 13:1–22. Amnon, the son of the king, was in love with his sister Tamar but as she was a virgin it was impossible for him to be alone with her. Finally feigning illness he persuaded his father, the king, to allow Tamar to feed him on his sickbed. The Bible:

> And Tamar took the bread she had prepared and brought it to her brother Amnon in his bedroom. But when she took it to him to eat, he grabbed her and said, 'Come to my bed with me, my sister.'
>
> 'Don't, my brother!' she said to him. 'Don't force me. Such a thing should not be done in Israel! Don't do this wicked thing. What about me? Where could I get rid of my disgrace? And what about you? You would be like one of the wicked fools in Israel. Please speak to the king; he will not keep me from being married to you.' But he refused to listen to her, and since he was stronger than she, he raped her. Then Amnon hated her with intense hatred. In fact, he hated her more than he had loved her.
>
> Amnon said to her. 'Get up and get out!'
>
> 'No!' she said to him. 'Sending me away would be a greater wrong than what you have already done to me.'
>
> But he refused to listen to her. He called his personal servant and said, 'Get this woman out of here and bolt the door after her.'

A clear case of brutal rape and incest. The Old Testament gives us a very clear insight into the sexual and criminal behaviour of man in those far off days and this insight shows us that Wilson is clearly wrong to suggest that the Jack the Ripper murders were the first crimes of a sexual nature, similar to those we are familiar with today or what he affirms was 'the increase of sexual crime towards the end of the nineteenth century' as though rape with or without murder had hardly existed before. This is manifestly untrue, and is almost as naïve a position as believing that sexual perversion is something new, perhaps yet another symptom or malady of modern man. It is all there in the Bible: homosexual rape, sodomy, sex with animals, gang rape, incest, murder and mutilation. Moses himself handed down the laws which said:

> Do not lie with a man as one lies with a woman; that is detestable. [Leviticus 18:22]
>
> If a man has sexual relations with an animal, he must be put to death, and you must kill the animal.
>
> If a woman approaches an animal to have sexual relations with it, kill both the woman and the animal. They must be put to death; their blood will be on their own head. [Leviticus 20:15–17]

It must follow that if such laws had to be passed then it was for the express purpose of stopping the people from indulging in such acts. The Old Testament law makers were, one assumes, not merely indulging their fantasies. Equally there were strict laws laid down governing cases of rape:

> If a man happens to meet in a town a virgin pledged to be married and he sleeps with her, you shall take both of them to the gate of that town and stone them to death – the girl because she was in a town and did not scream for help, and the man because he violated another man's wife. But if out in the country a man happens to meet a girl pledged to be married and rapes her, only the man who has done this shall die. Do nothing to the girl; she has committed no sin deserving death. This case is like that of someone who

> attacks and murders his neighbour, for the man found the girl out in the country, and though the betrothed girl screamed, there was no-one to rescue her. If a man happens to meet a virgin who is not pledged to be married and rapes her and they are discovered, he shall pay the girl's father fifty shekels of silver. He must marry the girl, for he has violated her. He can never divorce her as long as he lives. [Deuteronomy 22:23–9)

Again it must follow that if laws had to be passed to protect women against rape then rape must have been of common occurrence. The Hittites – 1680 BC – also viewed rape and bestiality as capital offences plus there is a single fragmentary account from this time which appears to record the rape and murder of a child and the subsequent trial of the killer.[17] There is also substantial evidence from the Egyptian sixth dynasty – circa 2,500 BC – that homosexual rape was considered to be a fate worse than death and was commonly practised on captors after battle.[18] No, sexual crime is nothing new, it has been with us in every step of our evolution.

But perhaps the weakest aspect of Wilson's theory that the sexual criminal is somehow a product of our new age – and in particular he means serial killers like Jack the Ripper – is that he has not taken into account the massive and rapid advances in communication systems which took place in the same period as he is writing about. This is much like a man who has got the ticket but has anyway missed the train. For the unprecedented growth of the media since the middle of the nineteenth century – pony express, telegraph, telephone, radio, television and now instant communication throughout the world by satellite – has surely played a pivotal role in the rise of sexual crime, or better said in the *reporting* of that sexual crime. Today we, like millions of other people all over the world, can pick up our morning newspaper or switch on the television and read or hear about a murder that has taken place half an hour before on the other side of the planet.

Even the crimes of Jack the Ripper were headline news in America soon after they happened. If the crimes had taken place 400 years before it is unlikely that a person living in Portsmouth, seventy miles away from London, would have ever heard about them. Equally so the mass murderer Pedro Alonzo Lopez was able to go on a spree of rape and murder between 1978 and 1980 which accounted for 350 young girls before he was apprehended. This was because he operated in a remote area of Ecuador populated by native Indians with little or no communication network. If he had carried out the crimes in Central London in the same years there is no doubt he would have been caught a lot quicker. This is the point, the rapid rise of communication systems and the consequent rise in the establishment of and improvement in policing methods in the same period that Wilson is talking about has made life harder for the serial killer or any other type of criminal than ever before. But it has made the reporting of their crimes easier, so we know about them.

The situation, in fact, could be the exact reverse of what Wilson claims and that 500 years ago there could have been more 'sexual criminals' and crimes than there are today. A Ripper could have travelled through a country 500 years ago, or even several countries, raping and murdering and the inhabitants would have believed each murder to have been a separate unrelated event because they did not possess the means to communicate with one another that we have today. The final message of this is that we should really be writing a book about Pedro Lopez who raped and murdered 350 young girls rather than a book about an unknown who murdered less than a dozen women. The reason we are not is the massive influence of today's media. We all know of Jack the Ripper's crimes but who ever heard of Pedro Lopez?

It is tempting to go further into the subject of 'sex crime' – and we will to a certain extent in a later chapter in an attempt to build up a profile of Jack the Ripper – but the subject is colossal and not in the scope of this work, but hopefully we may be at the stage where we are able to view the crimes of Jack the Ripper *without* the prejudice of assuming that the murders were the 'first sex crimes in our modern sense of the word'.

Rather than sitting back and allowing our Ripperologists to dominate the theoretical scene completely, let us for once go on the attack. Let us develop a line of thought – no matter how ridiculous it may seem at the start – that they regard as untenable. Reach right into an area of the Ripper's possible motives which they, as a group, dismiss out of hand. In his psychological portrait of Jack the Ripper Wilson claims that the earlier popular belief that the Ripper could have been a religious maniac with a murderous bent for killing prostitutes is highly unlikely.[19] But can we be so sure in dismissing religious mania as a possible motive for the Jack the Ripper murders?

There were some very strange characters running around the streets of Whitechapel in 1888. Aaron Kosminski was a typical example, a Polish Jewish hairdresser – and incidentally a man three 'Ripperologists' have set their money on as being the Ripper or at least a link to him[20] – who was regularly hauled off to the lunatic asylum where on one occasion the doctor who certified him said: 'He declared that he is guided and his movements altogether controlled by an instinct that informs his mind, he says that he knows the movements of all mankind, he refuses food from others because he is told to do so, and he eats out of the gutter for the same reason.'[21] But more of Aaron Kosminski later. It is now necessary to look in detail at the murder of Mary Jane Kelly.

5 Sacrificial Lambs

Sometimes he thought sadly to himself, 'Why?' and sometimes he thought, 'Wherefore?' and sometimes he thought, 'Inasmuch as which?'

Mary Jane Kelly was murdered – on Friday 9 November at Miller's Court, Dorset Street – in the most horrible circumstances that can be imagined. Although it was never the intention of this book to go into the gruesome details of the Ripper murders, there are some very curious points about Kelly's death that deserve to be mentioned in fair pursuit of the Ripper, and his possible motives. Out of the four, five or six victims of the Ripper, Mary Jane Kelly was without a doubt the most badly mutilated, but even that word fails to convey the almost total destruction of her body which seemed to have been the murderer's intention. Suffice to say that one of the doctors, Dr Bond, who was called to inspect her remains, afterwards suffered years of insomnia and depression and finally threw himself out of a window in 1901.

To fully understand the horror of what was visited on Mary Jane Kelly on that November night in 1888 it is necessary to look at the reports given by eyewitnesses and other sources at the time:

> She had been completely disembowelled, and her entrails had been taken out and placed on the table ... The woman's nose had been cut off, and her face gashed and mutilated so that it was quite beyond recognition. Both her

> breasts too had been cut clean away and placed by the side of her liver and other entrails on the table.
> (John MacCarthy, landlord of Miller's Court, where Kelly was murdered)[1]

> We are able to state, on good authority, that notwithstanding all that has been said to the contrary, a portion of the body organs was missing.
> *(Daily Telegraph* 13 November 1888)

> The throat had been cut right across with a knife, nearly severing the head from the body. The abdomen had been partially ripped open, and both of the breasts had been cut from the body, the left arm, like the head, hung to the body by the skin only. The nose had been cut off, the forehead skinned, and the thighs down to the feet, stripped of the flesh. The abdomen had been slashed with a knife across downwards, and the liver and entrails wrenched away. The entrails and other portions of the frame were missing, but the liver, etc, it is said, were found placed between the feet of the poor victim. The flesh from the thighs and legs, together with the breasts and nose, had been placed by the murderer on the table, and one of the hands of the dead woman had been pushed in her stomach.
> *(Illustrated Police News* 17 November 1888)

All in all a gruesome sight, and no wonder Dr Bond never recovered from the experience. One only needs to take a quick glance at the photographs showing the remains of what used to be Mary Jane Kelly to understand the overwhelming horror that the discoverers of her body must have felt. But the photographs of Kelly taken at the time do show that there are some inconsistencies in the reports. The flesh from her cheeks is also missing and it is only Kelly's right thigh that has been stripped down to the bone.

Another statement from John MacCarthy illustrates the horror of that night only too well:

> The sight we saw I cannot drive away from my mind. It looked more like the work of the devil than of a man. I had heard a great deal about the Whitechapel murders, but I declare to God I had never expected to see such a sight as this. The whole scene is more than I can describe. I hope I may never see such a sight as this again.[2]

MacCarthy felt it was the work of the 'devil' and declared to 'God' that he had never expected to see such a sight, but in hindsight perhaps he should have rather appealed to the 'devil', for the terrible crime that was committed on Mary Jane Kelly that night in 1888 may have had some very ancient precedents. Precedents that go back as far as the history of man has been recorded, as written down in the book of man's origins and beliefs: the Bible. But before attempting to demonstrate this curious connection between the murder of a prostitute in Whitechapel in 1888 and a holy book with its origins in the mists of time, it is necessary to summarize the peculiar mutilations carried out on Kelly's body by her murderer:

1 Her throat was slit.
2 The breasts, nose and flesh from the right thigh had all been cut away and placed on a table.
3 An attempt had been made to detach the left arm.
4 The abdomen had been cut open, the entrails and other portions of the frame had been removed and were not found. The liver had also been taken out but was found between her legs (or on the table, according to different witnesses).
5 Lastly mention must be made of the very important fact that the murderer had at some time during the killing and mutilation of Kelly lit a fire in the grate that had burnt so fiercely that it had melted the handle of a nearby kettle. A fire that was still warm seven hours after the discovery of her body.

The majority of writers have seen this killing as random

carnage, carried out by a killer in a fury of blood lust, and there is no doubt that it was the work of a maniac, but a maniac with a peculiar system and, believe it or not, a maniac who was following, almost exactly, a ritual for slaughter that was laid down in the time of Moses and others.

It is now time to quote the relevant passages from the Bible and to compare them to the five points mentioned above.

> Take from this ram the fat, the fat tail, the fat around the inner parts, the covering of the liver, both kidneys with the fat on them, and the right thigh …
>
> (Exodus 29:22–33)

> From the fellowship offering he is to bring a sacrifice made to the Lord by fire: all the fat that covers the inner parts or is connected to them, both kidneys with the fat on them near the loins, and the covering of the liver, which he will remove with the kidneys. Then Aaron's sons are to burn it on the altar on top of the burnt offering that is on the burning wood, as an offering made by fire, an aroma pleasing to the Lord.
>
> (Leviticus 3:3–5)

> He slaughtered the ox and the ram as the fellowship offering for the people. His sons handed him the blood, and he sprinkled it against the altar on all sides. But the fat portions of the ox and the ram – the fat tail, the layer of fat, the kidneys and the covering of the liver – these they laid on the breasts, and then Aaron burned the fat on the altar. Aaron waved the breasts and the right thigh before the Lord as a wave offering as Moses commanded.
>
> (Leviticus 9:18–22)

Obviously we are discussing the ritual slaughter of animals here as opposed to humans, but that is not the point. The point is that we have here a ritual that describes the slaughter of a living creature to an exact degree. The inner parts are removed, the 'fat that covers the inner parts or is connected to them, both kidneys, the covering of the liver' are removed and burnt. The liver is not burnt. The right thigh and breasts are removed, but not burnt. Using other original sources we are able to follow this ancient ritual even further. From the 'Temple Scroll 11QT:ii–xxiv' (one of the Dead Sea Scrolls):

> Behold, I will make a covenant. For it is something dreadful I will do to you ... This is what you shall offer on the altar ... they shall offer to Y H W H the right thigh of the ram ... as a holocaust and the fat covering the entrails and the two kidneys and the fat on them and on the loins and the whole fat tail close to the backbone and the appendage of the liver ... This is a holocaust, an offering by fire, of soothing odour before Y H W H. They shall burn everything on the altar over the holocaust to complete their ordination ... He shall offer on the altar and burn the fat ... all the fat on the entrails and the appendage of the liver and the two kidneys ... They shall offer to Y H W H an offering from the rams and the lambs, the right thigh, the breast, the cheeks, the stomach and the foreleg as far as the shoulder bone, and they shall wave them as a wave offering. The priest's portions shall be the thigh of the offering and the breast ... the forelegs, the cheeks and the stomachs as an eternal rule, from the children of Israel and the shoulder remaining of the foreleg shall be for the Levites ... They shall take away ... the right thigh and the breast ... the cheeks and stomach shall be the priest's portion ... The High Priest shall offer the holocaust of the Levites first, and afterwards he shall send up in smoke the holocaust of the tribe of Judah ...[3]

Compare this to the five points we listed earlier associated with Kelly's death. The right thigh of Kelly was stripped of flesh to the bone, the breasts were removed, the innards were taken out with the kidneys and somehow destroyed or taken away, but the liver was left intact, the flesh of her face was removed, her left arm (her foreleg) was removed as far as the shoulder bone … and it seems highly likely that the killer lit the fire to burn the missing parts of her body. The killer laid the breasts, nose and the flesh from her thigh carefully on the table and he placed her liver either between her legs or again on the table in accordance with the instructions in the ritual. 'Behold, I will make a covenant. For it is something dreadful I will do to you … '

Prophetic words from a book of prophets, for what happened to Mary Jane Kelly was indeed a dreadful thing. But then her killer wouldn't have seen it like that at all, if he did carry out the murder of Kelly according to the slaughter ritual repeated at least four times in the Bible, then he must have been familiar with the holy book and its recommendations as to the treatment of prostitutes.

In a letter supposedly from the hands of Jack the Ripper himself, the writer says that he has 'a down on whores and shan't quit ripping them apart till I do get bucked'. A 'down on whores' was nothing new in 1888. Ezekiel had a similar 'down on whores' in about 600 BC as is evident from his writings in an address to Oholibah the prostitute: 'I will direct my jealous anger against you, and they will deal with you in a fury. They will cut off your noses and ears, and those of you who are left will fall by the sword … ' (Ezekiel 23:25–26)

Remember Kelly's nose was removed. The Ripper also wrote in the same letter that he would 'clip the lady's ears off' and he certainly tried to do just that when he murdered another victim, Catherine Eddowes. But let us return to our Old Testament prophet, Ezekiel:

> Therefore, you prostitute, hear the word of the Lord! This is what the Sovereign Lord says: Because you poured out your lust and exposed your nakedness in your promiscuity with your lovers … therefore I am going to gather all your lovers, with whom you found pleasure, those you loved as well as those you hated. I will gather them against you

> from all around and will strip you in front of them, and they will all see your nakedness. I will sentence you to the punishment of women who commit adultery and who shed blood: I will bring upon you the blood vengeance of my wrath and jealous anger. Then I will hand you over to your lovers, and they will ... strip you of your clothes and take your fine jewellery and leave you naked and bare. They will bring a mob against you, who will stone you and hack you to pieces with their swords ... and inflict punishment on you in the sight of many women. I will put a stop to your prostitution ... Then my wrath against you will subside and my jealous anger will turn away from you; I will be calm and no longer angry.'
>
> (Ezekiel 16:35–43)

And:

> But righteous men will sentence them to the punishment of women who commit adultery and shed blood, because they are adulterous and blood is on their hands.
>
> [Ezekiel 23:45)

Ezekiel even praised the weapons to be used in such a slaughter and dictated their use:

> A sword, a sword, sharpened and polished – sharpened for slaughter, polished to flash like lightning! – The sword is appointed to be polished, to be grasped with the hand; it is sharpened and polished, made ready for the hand of the slayer ... Let the sword strike twice, even three times. It is a sword for slaughter – a sword for great slaughter ... Oh! It is made to flash like lightning, it is grasped for slaughter. O sword, slash to the right, then to the left, wherever your blade is turned. I too will strike my hands together and my wrath will subside. I the Lord have spoken.
>
> (Ezekiel 21:9–18)

The prophet Ezekiel's down on 'whores' is shared by writers of the New Testament and we are assured in Hebrews (10:22) as a general rule that: 'In fact, the law requires that nearly everything be cleansed with blood, and without the shedding of blood there is no forgiveness.' A sentiment that a Ripper with a 'down on whores' would no doubt have sympathized with, especially when he was specifically told in Colossians (3:5) that he should: 'Put to death, therefore, whatever belongs to your earthly nature: sexual immorality, impurity, evil desires and greed, which is idolatry.'

Corinthians 6:13–17 also has words of succour for those with a 'down on whores':

> The body is not meant for sexual immorality, but for the Lord, and the Lord for the body. By his power God raised the Lord from the dead, and he will raise us also. Do you not know that your bodies are members of Christ himself? Shall I then take the members of Christ and unite them with a prostitute? Never! Do you not know that he who unites himself with a prostitute is one with her body?

Revelations 2:20–3 shows quite clearly how prostitutes should be dealt with by a 'good' and 'pure' follower of the faith: 'You tolerate that woman Jezebel ... she misleads my servants into sexual immorality ... I have given her time to repent of her immorality but she is unwilling. So I will cast her on a bed of suffering, and I will make those who commit adultery with her suffer intensely ... '

'The beast and the ten horns you saw will hate the prostitute. They will bring her to the ruin and leave her naked; they will eat her flesh and burn her with fire.' (Revelations 17:16)

'She [the prostitute] has become a home for demons and a haunt for every evil spirit ... Give her as much torture and grief as the glory and luxury she gave herself.' (Revelations 18:2–8)

Powerful words of hate and destruction, words that justify any believer to have a 'down on whores', to 'cast them on a bed of suffering' and to give the whores 'much torture and grief', to 'shed their blood' by 'hacking them to pieces' and 'cutting off their nose' with his 'sword, polished for great slaughter' and to 'strike twice, or even three times'. He is justified, he knows that, for he is assured by the book that 'the body is not meant for sexual immorality' and it must be 'put to death' for he knows that 'without the shedding of blood there is no forgiveness'. Here is a recipe for murder, and no mistake.

The importance of this digression into Biblical rituals and attitudes is that it not only dramatically illustrates how some of the experts can deliberately mislead their readers in the case of Jack the Ripper, because there is an obvious connection between the ritualized murder and mutilation of Mary Jane Kelly and the Mosaic sacrificial laws. Much more importantly it shows that Jack the Ripper was a very particular type of killer and our suspect from the earlier chapters, Michael Kidney, does not fit this profile at all. To try and come closer to the Ripper it is now necessary to look at the behaviour of other criminals and the horde of suspects that the Ripperologists confront us with.

6 Suspects

'Why, what's happened to your tail?' he said in surprise.
'What has happened to it?' said Eeyore.
'It isn't there!'
'Are you sure?'
'Well, either a tail is there, or it isn't there. You can't make a mistake about it. And yours isn't there.'

To peer through, or even into the host of Jack the Ripper suspects – an incredible 139 different candidates according to the latest Ripper volume[1]– is a daunting task that can only lead to defeat if one is really serious about trying to track down the killer. A lifetime's work of false trails leading to nowhere in dusty reading rooms. When the sheer size of the market in potential suspects is considered one can only throw their hands up in the air in despair and deep dismay, then move quickly onto a mystery which might at least offer the chance of a solution.

And this is what the whole game of name Jack the Ripper is about. The Ripperologists don't know who Jack the Ripper was either but they are on fairly sure ground when they assume it must have been someone who was actually living in London in 1888 whose name has come down to us with history, whether it be a statesman, doctor or a fish gutter doesn't matter, all that is important is the name. All these names are thrown into a hat and one can peer in and say 'yes, in there is the name of Jack the

Ripper' ... and the more names the better. The principle being that if you are given three darts to hit the bull's-eye you'll probably fail but if you've got 139 to throw away then chances are you'll be on target at least once.

It is an almost hopeless situation where the real facts are rare and speculation is rife. As we have seen some authors are prepared to base their theories on the speculations of someone who is an admitted liar, and this speculation then goes on to become the basis for a world-wide bestseller on the subject but nevertheless the author is acclaimed by fellow Ripperologists as holding 'an honoured place in the annals of Ripper research'. This is exactly what happened in the case of Stephen Knight's book *Jack the Ripper: The Final Solution* with its anti-authoritarian and anti-masonic themes. The claims that the Ripper murders were a Freemasonry conspiracy carried out by Prince Albert Victor, Lord Salisbury and Sir William Gull make riveting reading, it is true, but as we already saw in the first chapter the claims are based purely on information from Joseph Sickert, the artist, who claims his grandmother, Annie Crook, was married to Prince Albert Victor. As the editors of *The Jack the Ripper A to Z* point out in the strongest terms, stories coming from Mr Sickert should be treated with a good deal of caution.[2]

This point of view can only be sympathized with in view of Joseph Sickert's claims made in national newspapers in 1984 that the *Yorkshire* Ripper had attempted to murder him.[3] Clearly there is a large element of fiction and fantasy involved in the entire Sickert and Knight affair as Sickert himself confirmed in an article in the *Sunday Times* in 1977 where he admitted that the whole thing was a hoax. Unfortunately it is a sad fact of life today that the book market is much like the newspaper market and to sell it is necessary to have headlines that scream out some outrageous plot at its readers. If our Jack the Ripper does prove to be a lowly labourer or fish porter then nobody is going to take a blind bit of notice, but if we can come up with a belted Earl or something similar and weave a complete and utter fantastic story around him with the required amount of gore, sex and violence thrown in then we can sit back and bathe in the glory of yet another 'final solution'. Facts or the truth do not matter anymore, it seems, in the solution of the Ripper mystery. It is an open market.

This is obvious from the latest volumes that have appeared recently about Jack the Ripper. *Murder and Madness, The Secret Life of Jack the Ripper Based on Heretofore Unrevealed Information from Scotland Yard* by Dr David Abrahamsen.[4] It is a bewildering tale by a forensic scientist – he is described as a leading expert on the criminal mind – which has Prince Albert Victor Edward and his tutor J.K. Stephen running around Whitechapel in drag taking out their sexual resentments against prostitutes by ripping them to pieces. Dr Abrahamsen does not produce one single piece of evidence to substantiate his wild claims, apart from the noteworthy facts that J.K. Stephen smoked a pipe and Prince Albert was in the habit of dressing in collar and cuffs. If this forensic scientist had bothered to check his facts he would have rapidly found out, from the court circulars of the time he is writing about, that Prince Albert was out of London in the company of friends and family on every single occasion that the Ripper struck. If that's not bad enough he then delves deeply into the subject of sex crime and his somewhat flippant speculations about the subject leave one cold and frightened. Frightened that a forensic scientist can honestly believe this sort of stuff in the 1990s. He claims that many men who have sex with prostitutes are doing so because of an infantile fixation with their mothers, and that many prostitutes ply their trade as revenge against a weak father figure.

In fact the Hite Report on Male Sexuality shows that most men are quite honest about their reasons for commercial sex, and various straightforward reasons are given for having sex with prostitutes: to gain sexual experience, to lose their virginity, to gain sexual independence and because of the chances it offered for uninvolved emotionless sex. Other men found it too unemotional and never repeated the experience and the vast majority of men seemed to find that having sex with a prostitute was no different than wining and dining a date to get her into bed.

Regarding his comments about prostitutes revenging themselves on weak fathers perhaps he would do well to visit Prague and question the thousands of young girls that have flocked into the city to sell their bodies. It is the only way to earn a living in their economically devastated country.

Abrahamsen regards sexual perversion as an erotic expression of hate with perverted sexual behaviour being the result of psychological castration – whatever that means – and classifies certain homosexual behaviour as a perversion. He might be interested to know that between 43 and 48 per cent of all males have had sexual relations of some kind with another male while a teenager or a boy.

After assuring his readers that they all possess the impulse to kill he then links the sexual drive (supposedly in both sexes) to emotions of hate and murder, as though biological reproduction and pure pleasure have nothing to do with the urge to copulate.

Worse is to come. The prostitutes, he continues, that were so viciously mutilated and slaughtered by the Ripper were secretly attracted to the maniac with a knife. Why? Well it is obvious when you think about it. As he explains it the Ripper had already killed some of their kind and when something like this happens to a prostitute then the others just flock around begging to be cut apart and murdered. His startling theories are matched by his sexual knowledge. The reader is informed that homosexuals indulge in anal intercourse and often wear women's clothes as this triggers orgasm. Perhaps the key that really unlocks Abrahamsen's secret door to the solution of the Ripper mystery is when he points out that the wonderful fairy tale, Sleeping Beauty is nothing less than a necrophiliac's fantasy.

The Ripper and the Royals by Melvyn Fairclough[5] is yet another extension of Stephen Knight's book, again based largely on evidence supplied by Joseph Sickert. But this one has HRH Duke of Clarence, Lord Randolph Churchill, Sir William Gull, J.K. Stephen and coach driver John Netley carrying out the bloody murders in yet another Freemason conspiracy. The plot reaches right from 1888 to today with national newspapers, Special Branch detectives, Crown Prosecution Service and the Yorkshire Ripper all involved in the elaborate plot. The secret diaries of Inspector Abberline are revealed to the author but not the reader and very senior police chiefs of the time act as look-outs for the killers. One can visualize the scene as the Duke of Clarence and Lord Randolph Churchill, covered in blood, creep past the hundreds of police constables stationed in Whitechapel: 'Evening your Highness … evening my Lord.' The Duke of Clarence lives on after his death, as does Mary Kelly and the Royal Ripper looks set to be the final solution to end all final solutions. All well and good, but again one has to question the author's motives in including the revolting photographs of the Ripper's victims. The reproduction of Catherine Eddowes' picture showing her naked, brutalized and propped up against a wall is bad enough but why include the already widely circulated picture of the remains of Mary Kelly, legs spread wide displaying her ripped and bloody reproductive organs.

Is there a way out of this dreadful morass that threatens to engulf any serious effort to discover the identity of Jack the Ripper? Possibly, just possibly. If, from the very start, one is prepared to establish well accepted criteria in known criminal behaviour – particularly in what we now term as 'serial murder' cases – and to re-examine what the last hundred years should have taught us about the activities of such criminals then it might be possible to apply these lessons to the case of Jack the Ripper. Surely with the increase of our knowledge into these types of crimes – through increasingly sophisticated police and forensic techniques – we must be in a better situation to solve this mystery than ever before? Surely the unique insight that we now possess into the workings of the human mind, particularly that of criminals and more particularly that of murderers, must mean we are closer and not further away from the truth of the matter? The only stumbling block must be the wild theories of the Ripperologists and it is for this reason that they must be ignored at the start of this journey into the unknown. Later it will be necessary to consider their various theories.

One of the first points that confronts anybody looking into cases of murder, particularly serial murder, is that a large number of the actual killers would have been interviewed as suspects by police investigating the murder but would eventually be ruled out for a variety of reasons. Only later when confronted by overwhelming evidence – usually obtained by luck – would the police realize that this was in fact their man. This holds true for some of the most notorious mass murderers of all time.

Peter Sutcliffe, the 'Yorkshire Ripper', and Ted Bundy, two of the best-known cases, have already been extensively covered in a previous chapter but there are a host of other murderers sharing this common factor. Robert Hansen was also mentioned earlier in another connection, and he was also interviewed by police investigating the killings of twenty women who had been hunted down and shot in the woods around Anchorage, Alaska. The local police were disinclined to really suspect Hansen because he was well known to all in Anchorage as a successful and respectable member of the business community. Later, however, when the police were desperate to catch the killer they contacted the FBI

Academy 'psychological profiling team' – who specialize in profiling just such mass murderers – and gave a description of the multiple murders, they were told by the FBI specialists that the killer was probably a respected member of the business community. This still, for reasons unknown, didn't result in Hansen's arrest and it was only when one of his victims eventually managed to escape – as Hansen was attempting to load her on his private airplane where he was going to throw her out without a parachute – and tell her story to the police that he was detained and eventually charged.

Raymond Morris was interviewed by police looking for the killer of several young girls in Staffordshire, England, in the mid 1960s but they were quickly satisfied with the alibi his wife provided. Later the number of his car was noted by a witness when Morris tried to drag another girl into his car and this time the police found child pornography in the house and were able to show that his wife was lying about her husband's movements. False alibis, usually supplied by family or close friends, are a painfully recurrent theme in these cases of brutal murder.

Van Zon murdered his way through Amsterdam and Holland in the mid 1960s – no one is really sure of his eventual toll – and he killed both men and women without compunction. He came to the attention of the Dutch police when his wife went to them and accused him of attempting to murder her. As he was already on probation for some other minor sexual offence they didn't take the accusation very seriously and merely locked him up for a month. After his release he carried straight on with his killings, and four more victims were to die before he was eventually arrested for almost killing a woman with a lead pipe by beating her around the skull.

One of the two 'Hillside Stranglers', Bianchi, was twice interviewed by the Los Angeles police in their efforts to end the reign of terror that claimed as many as ten young girls in the late 1970s. Two more girls were killed before the trail led back to Bianchi again.

The 'Boston Strangler', Albert De Salvo, had been in police custody and jailed for fairly minor sex offences – in other words he was well known to the Boston police. After the series of thirteen horrific rapes and murders between 1962 and 1964, however, the police were unable to make the connection between the killings and De Salvo, until someone finally remembered him from previous offences. Even then the police thought that De Salvo was only guilty of rape and it wasn't until he was admitted to a mental institute where he was diagnosed as schizophrenic and went on to confess to the murders in such detail that there could be no denying that De Salvo was indeed the 'Boston Strangler.'

In 1922 the local police of Dorset, England, carried out a murder investigation which still stands today as a shining example of how a murder should not be investigated. A woman's body was found in a field near to Boscombe. She had been beaten to death with a hammer and sexually assaulted. The most promising evidence was the imprint of a car tyre which was identified as a Dunlop Magnum on the nearside rear wheel and the testimony of a man who had seen a grey-green touring car driven by a man in chauffeur's uniform in the area. The police went on to interview every chauffeur in the Bournemouth area and eventually came to Thomas Allaway who drove a grey-green touring car for his employers. Three of the wheels of this car were indeed fitted with Dunlop Magnum tyres but the all important nearside rear wheel was fitted with a Michelin so the police asked Allaway if he had changed the tyre recently. When he replied no, the police went away quite happily accepting his alibi that he had been visiting the local pub at the time of the murder. Meanwhile a clerk at the local post office told the police that she remembered a chauffeur who had been sending telegrams to women asking them to catch the next train to Bournemouth. Allaway had lured his victim, Irene

Wilkins, down to Bournemouth with a telegram promising work. An engineer who had travelled down on the same train as the murder victim informed the police that he had seen her collected from the station by a chauffeur driving a grey-green touring car. This should have clinched the case by now but the police went on to display even more incompetence. The engineer, Frank Humphris, saw the same car again two weeks later and managed to get its number this time. But still the police didn't act. The clerk at the post office recognized the chauffeur – who was fond of sending telegrams to ladies – again six weeks later and followed him outside to take the number of his grey-green tourer. Still the police did nothing. Later the intrepid female clerk and her workmates showed more diligence than the police and followed the chauffeur home on his next visit and passed the information onto the police. Still nothing.

It was only when Allaway absconded from his employers with their cheque book and started passing dud cheques that he was arrested. Once in their custody even the police found it hard to defy the barrage of evidence that pointed towards Allaway as being the killer of Irene Wilkins and they checked out the car once again and found – lo and behold one wants to say – that the spare tyre was a Dunlop Magnum with good tread while the Michelin was practically worn through. Allaway had read about the tyre track left at the scene of the murder in the local paper and changed the tyre. Even with their powerful evidence the police still had trouble presenting a watertight case at court. It was only when Allaway was asked to write out the same words as appeared on the murder telegram and made the exact same three spelling mistakes that the jury knew they had their man.

As well as illustrating our theme that suspects who have been in the hands of the police at some time often ultimately prove to be the murderer this case is a classic example of a police system that was still in its infancy thirty-four years *after* the Ripper murders.

Six years after the Ripper murders France was to experience a similar spate of terrible crimes when a killer travelled the countryside strangling, raping and disembowelling young girls and castrating young boys. The killer's description was well known to the French police. He was described as having a twisted upper lip marked by a scar, a bloodshot right eye and of unkempt appearance with shaggy black beard and long hair. The killer attempted to attack a servant girl on a lonely road but a passing labourer managed to beat him off and later alerted the police. The police managed to capture this strange individual but after examining his identity papers allowed him to go free. The description of the man leaves no doubt – the disfigurement to his face must have been severe as he had shot himself in the face with a pistol – that he was an unusual-looking individual and he had just attempted to attack a girl. But the police let this strange man on his way and he went on to kill three more victims. Joseph Vacher was eventually taken into custody when he attempted to attack a large woman in a forest and had the tables turned on him.

As a fairly regular, but minor sexual offender, Colin Pitchfork was well known to the Leicester police and when two young girls were murdered in Enderby he was interviewed by police. They did not really suspect him but were carrying out routine investigations into all sexual offenders of the area in a process of elimination. His alibi and manner satisfied them and they closed his file as a suspect. If they had probed a little bit further they would have surely caught Colin Pitchfork before he went on to commit the second murder. For not only was he on police files as a sexual offender he had also been treated for his sexual disorder at the Carlton Hayes Hospital, outside of which the body of the first victim, Lynda Mann, was found. This connection should not have been missed by a modern police force in 1983, but it was. After the second murder Pitchfork was finally arrested after a friend admitted that he had stood in for Pitchfork, during the massive blood-testing operation the police carried out to find the killer.

Obviously it cannot be taken for granted that every murderer has been interviewed and subsequently released by the police because of a cast-iron alibi, or other reasons, and then later is shown to be the killer. But there is an awfully persuasive pattern in the murder investigations we have followed up to now, and make no mistake we are discussing some of the most infamous mass murderers of the last century. The pattern is clear: original police suspicions are lulled by a false alibi usually given by family or close friends, then later a piece of luck usually shows them that their suspicions were after all well-founded. One also has to say, sadly, that there seems to be a continuing pattern of police incompetence of murder investigation right through this century, sometimes – as in the case of the search for the killer driving a grey-green tourer with a Dunlop Magnum tyre – of an appalling level.

This then gives us our first criterion: that the Ripper was most probably a *named* suspect at some time in the investigation and had probably been interviewed by the police to eliminate him from the murder enquiry. But the above murder cases also give us another criterion which is equally well known from hundreds of other cases of serious crimes: that the Ripper probably did not start out his odious career with murder and mutilation but with lesser crimes – perhaps even very minor offences – and the police were very likely to have been aware of these crimes.

A curious component of criminal mentality – especially that of some serial killers – is the strange desire to be involved somehow with the investigations of their own crimes. Sometimes, they march boldly into a police station to complain about the inefficiency of the police officers investigating their own murder, or write long letters of accusation against various people totally unconnected with the crime, and sometimes even offering to help the police in their investigation. This behaviour sometimes results in the criminal revisiting the site of the murder and Colin Wilson feels that this is largely to gloat over their dead victims,[6] but this could be too simple an explanation. Wilson also believes that such serial killers are motivated to contact the police or others because of a suicidal element that is involved with sex crime but again this could be a gross over-simplification of the motives. This strange behaviour – both the revisiting of the site and the desire to be somehow involved in the investigation – could perhaps have its origins more in a combination of the powerful guilt mechanisms of the individuals concerned and an overpowering desire to be there on the 'pulse' of things. But no matter to the psychology of the behaviour, it suits our present purpose to know that it exists as a few examples will illustrate.

John Haigh was a classic example, walking into Chelsea police station with a woman on his arm in 1949 to report the disappearance of a woman that he had murdered two days earlier. To assist the police even further he gave them his business address where he had murdered Mrs Oliver Durand-Deacon and then melted her body down in a tub of acid. It didn't take the police long to realize that they had a mass murderer on their hands who specialized in killing people whose fortune he wanted to 'inherit'.

When the remains of two bodies were found in a stream in Scotland in 1935 the police and forensic experts really had their work cut out for them as the bodies had been hacked to pieces and the skin removed from the faces so that identification would be impossible. For the same reason the fingertips of one body were also removed. But when a wild, dishevelled man burst into a Lancaster police station to complain about the disappearance of his wife and police harassment – when there had been none – the police knew they had a suspect. Not satisfied with that performance the man, Dr Buck Ruxton, made another appearance at the station a few days later when he wept across the counter complaining that neighbours were spreading rumours that he had killed his wife and maid. Eventually the forensic trail also led back to him and he was finally successfully prosecuted for the murder of his wife and maid but many involved in the case remained convinced that if the doctor had not lost his nerve and gone whining to the police he would have got away with the double murder.

In 1946 Neville Heath took a woman to his London hotel room and in the course of a sadistic session – in which it seems the woman was a willing partner – lost control of himself and killed her. Then he travelled down to Bournemouth murdering another woman on the beach and explaining to yet another that a woman had been murdered by persons unknown in his hotel room in London. She advised him to go to the local police which he did, explaining to the astonished officials – who immediately recognized him from his description which had appeared in every national paper in the country – that he might be able to help them with their enquiry. He was not intending to confess, his offer of help seems to have been genuine enough from his own point of view as he had a few days after the first 'murder' written to the officer in charge of the investigation in London offering help and promising to supply the weapon that was used to mutilate the woman which he had found. He had also complained to others that a man capable of such a terrible act must be a 'sexual maniac'.

Graham Backhouse led the Bristol police a merry trail of murder and mayhem when he complained to them that he was the victim of a conspiracy to murder him. The police were impressed with the evidence of threatening phone calls and letters accusing Backhouse of various misdeeds and when his wife was blown up in his car – her own car had broken down – by a home-made bomb they were convinced that someone was indeed determined to murder Mr Backhouse and placed him under police protection. The first doubts must have crept into their minds when Graham Backhouse made an angry phone call demanding that the police be removed from his land. When a few days later the police were called back to Backhouse's farm it was to find a bleeding and wounded Backhouse and a neighbour dead on the floor. He claimed that the neighbour had attacked him, so he had shot him twice with a shotgun in the chest. Backhouse's explanation was that this was the man who had sent the letters, made the telephone calls and tried to blow him up in his car. At first the police were inclined to believe him, but the forensic experts called to the scene were not so easily convinced and believed that Backhouse had staged the attack and had, in fact, murdered his neighbour. They eventually went on to prove this and when it was found that Backhouse had increased the insurance premium on his wife from £50,000 to £100,000 a month before the car bomb attack they knew they had their man and his motive. It is obvious that if Backhouse had not demanded the police to withdraw their protection and then gone on to murder his neighbour, things would have cooled down. He would also have been allowed to raise the money he needed in a more conventional manner, but he implicated himself by complaining about the police who were there to supposedly protect him.

Deeply religious and a member of an organization, the Alliance of Honour, that demanded of its members purity in body as well as mind, Norman Thorne nevertheless murdered and mutilated his fiancée, Elsie Cameron, in 1924 on his chicken farm in Sussex. She had tried to force him into marriage by claiming to be pregnant from him, while he maintained that they had never had sexual intercourse, and he was anyway in love with another. So he murdered his fiancée, dismembered her and buried her in the soil one of his chicken coops. Seven days later he presented himself at the local police station and expressed his desire to assist them in every way he could in the search for his missing fiancée. Later he had a photo taken of him standing in the very chicken coop where his fiancée was buried while the police looked on.

Dr Thomas Neill Cream was a legendary example of a murderer who just couldn't leave his wicked deeds to die like his poisoned victims in 1891. He murdered his prostitute victims almost long-distance as it were, by giving them small bottles of 'medicine' to take later. He then proceeded to write letters to all and sundry accusing a variety of public figures of the murders. He even marched into Scotland Yard on one occasion and demanded that the police stop following him, which they weren't, and there is no doubt about the fact that when he was hanged in 1892 he had put the rope round his neck himself.

The final case is perhaps the most audacious out of the lot and concerns a murderer who became known as the 'Zodiac' killer because he always used the symbol of the Zodiac when communicating with the police about his crimes. Between 1968 and 1969 'Zodiak' shot or stabbed a number of victims killing five of them and almost every time he had just killed someone, he directly phoned the San Francisco police to tell them where they could find the bodies and then ranted and raved at them for their incompetence and inefficiency in catching the killer!

So as can be seen there is yet another criterion which could possibly point to the identity of Jack the Ripper. Someone who acted in a similar fashion, presenting themselves to the police to offer assistance, berating the police for their incompetence, complaining of police harassment or writing strange letters to the press or people in authority.

Using these main criteria we will attempt to profile the suspects that are left after winnowing the Ripperologists pack of 139 down to a reasonable number by a process of radical elimination. But before doing that there are several other factors of modern murder investigation to be considered which may be of great help later.

The FBI Psychological Profiling Unit believe that in many cases of mutilation murder the more vicious the mutilation, particularly to the face of the victim, the closer the relationship between murderer and victim. Remember the post-mortem report on Mary Jane Kelly where it was detailed that her face was almost totally devoid of flesh. Sir Melville Leslie MacNaghten, the chief constable of Scotland Yard CID shortly after the Ripper murders, made the important observation about the murders that the 'fury of the mutilations *increased* in each case' and this is indeed a most crucial observation.

Another point that emerges from modern police hunts for serial killers is that as the police operation gains momentum, the killer has less and less room in which to move. As the hunt intensifies the killer's territory becomes squeezed and he is forced to operate in ever decreasing circles until he either stops murdering, moves away, commits suicide, gives himself up, or starts to murder on his own doorstep. The 'Jack the Stripper' murders of the mid 1960s are a classic example of this. The killer left his victims, strangled and naked, in the River Thames. It was obvious that the killer was committing the crimes elsewhere and then dumping the bodies. However, police activity became so intense in the killer's area that he was forced to dump his last victim at the actual murder site – his place of work. He then went on to commit suicide as the police had tightened the net to such an extreme that he knew he was about to be apprehended and furthermore had absolutely no chance of ensnaring more victims. His murderous career was well and truly over. This must have been even more so for Jack the Ripper than for the serial killer today, because he did not possess the easy mobility that we do now. The modern serial killer often makes use of the motorway systems available today in most countries and this makes him damn difficult to catch. But the Ripper was probably confined to foot and as the police net drew closer round him he may have been forced to kill increasingly nearer to his home base.

Chief Inspector Walter Dew, famous as the detective who arrested Crippen, was personally involved with only one of the Ripper murders – that of Mary Jane Kelly – but in his book *I Caught Crippen* he also made a valuable observation concerning the Ripper and his victims. He was amazed that the prostitutes of the Whitechapel area even after the horrific murder of Annie Chapman proved to be such easy targets for the killer and he posed the question: 'Is it feasible that there was something about him which placed him above suspicion?' The answer to his question must surely be yes. Though in saying so we mustn't forget the impoverished circumstances of the Ripper's victim. In every case – excepting perhaps that of Long Liz Stride – the women were forced to go out on the streets late at night to try and earn the four pence by selling their bodies to pay for their bed for the night. Mary Jane Kelly was killed in her room that is true, but it shouldn't be forgotten that she was months behind with her rent and on the point of being turned out of her lodgings. In other words she was also a very desperate woman. This is an important point to note and it's likely that the woman killed by the Ripper were more concerned about securing their four pence than over the appearance of their potential customer. Extreme poverty produces people who are prepared to take extreme risks. But that doesn't rule out the point that Inspector Dew raises. It would have certainly been easier for the Ripper if he had been someone above suspicion, a familiar face to the Dorset Street prostitutes, the boyfriend of someone they all knew, a policeman, or someone who was prepared to help them out with a few pence when they were down. It is certainly tempting to think that this could have been the case, and the important statement of the FBI that the more vicious the mutilation the closer the relationship between killer and victim, plus Sir Melville MacNaghten's observation that the 'fury of the mutilations increased in each case' also leads one in that direction. This then is another of our criteria: to look for someone whose position or relationship (to the victims) would allow him to carry out the murders without undue difficulty.

Finally to the Ripper himself. What sort of man should we be looking for? Has one hundred years intensive study into the criminal mind brought us closer to being able to identify the type of killer the Ripper was? Perhaps. If one studies similar cases that have occurred since Jack the Ripper then certainly different types of killers are easily recognizable. There appear to be four distinct types of killer in these serial murders. One is the full-blown psychotic, a chronic paranoid schizophrenic, who hears voices ordering him to kill, voices from demons or other strange sources like in one case from 'Jesus Christ and Company'. Herb Mullin killed over a dozen people in California in the early 1970s because voices had told him to do it and he assured his captors that it was Satan himself who was behind the deeds. The 'Son of Sam', David Berkowitz, who killed six people and wounded another seven in random shootings in new York during 1976 was similarly driven by the voices of demons. Peter Sutcliffe, the 'Yorkshire Ripper' also claimed that demons had been behind his vicious murders. The mass murderer and cannibal Albert Fish who claimed to have murdered 400 children in the USA between 1910 and 1934 had been suffering from delusions for years where voices had been urging him to kill. Fish is an important case as it shows that the full-blown maniac can appear to be quite normal, so normal that one of the psychiatrists, Frederick Wertham, who examined him in jail described him thus: 'a meek and innocuous little old man, gentle and benevolent, friendly and polite. If you wanted someone to entrust your children to, he would be the one you would

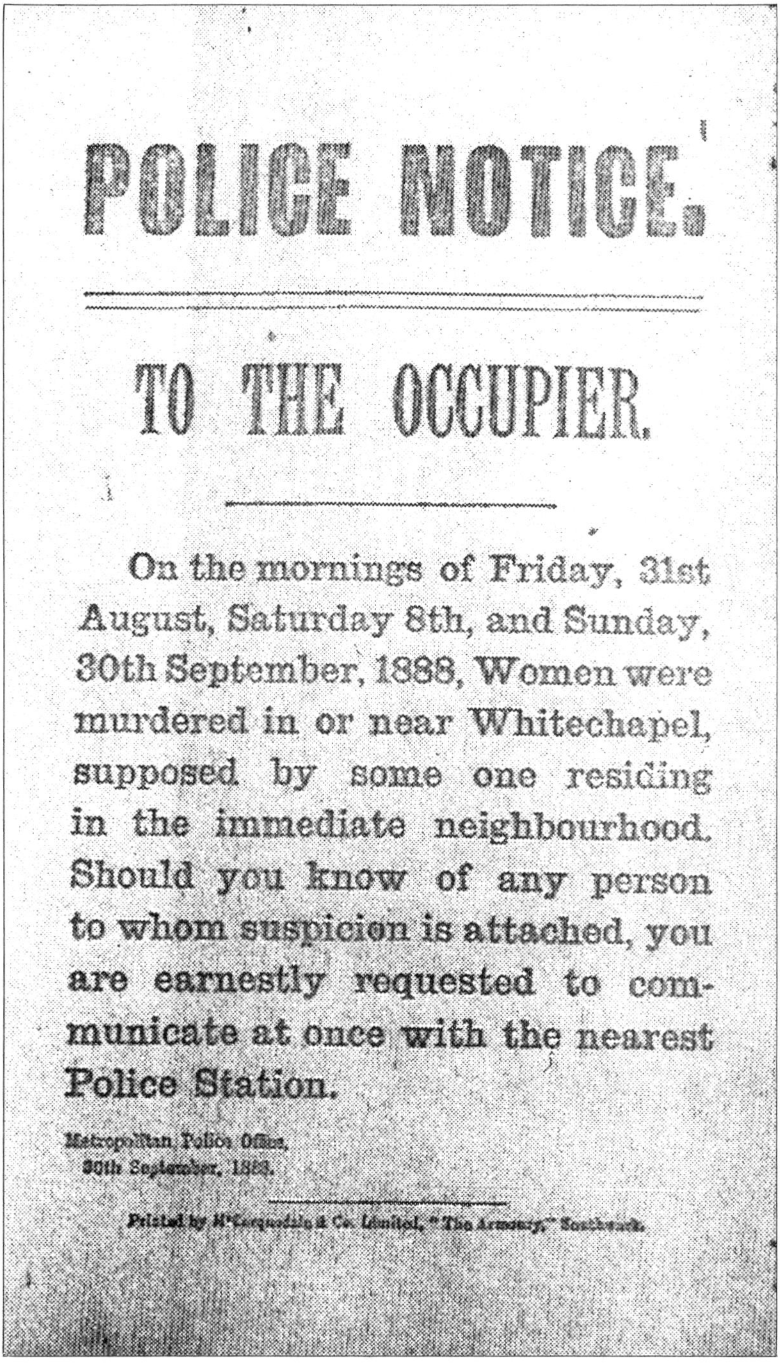

POLICE NOTICE.

TO THE OCCUPIER.

On the mornings of Friday, 31st August, Saturday 8th, and Sunday, 30th September, 1888, Women were murdered in or near Whitechapel, supposed by some one residing in the immediate neighbourhood. Should you know of any person to whom suspicion is attached, you are earnestly requested to communicate at once with the nearest Police Station.

Metropolitan Police Office,
30th September, 1888.

Printed by M'Corquodale & Co. Limited, "The Armoury," Southwark.

Metropolitan Police handbill produced during the intensive hunt for the Ripper in 1888

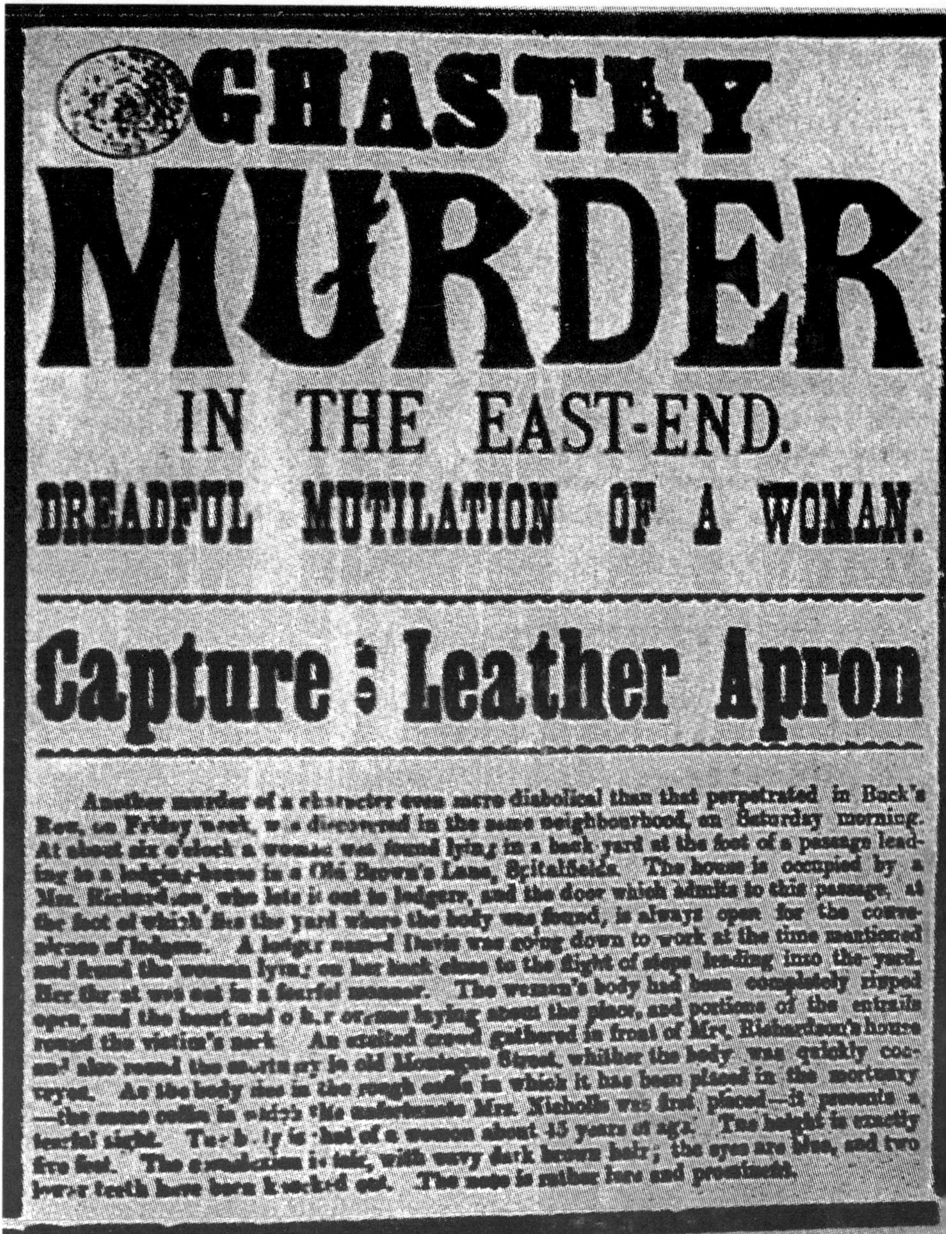

GHASTLY

MURDER

IN THE EAST-END.

DREADFUL MUTILATION OF A WOMAN.

Capture : Leather Apron

Another murder of a character even more diabolical than that perpetrated in Buck's Row, on Friday week, was discovered in the same neighbourhood, on Saturday morning. At about six o'clock a woman was found lying in a back yard at the foot of a passage leading to a lodging-house in a Old Brown's Lane, Spitalfields. The house is occupied by a Mrs. Richardson, who lets it out to lodgers, and the door which admits to this passage, at the foot of which lies the yard where the body was found, is always open for the convenience of lodgers. A lodger named Davis was going down to work at the time mentioned and found the woman lying on her back close to the flight of steps leading into the yard. Her throat was cut in a fearful manner. The woman's body had been completely ripped open, and the heart and other organs laying about the place, and portions of the entrails round the victim's neck. An excited crowd gathered in front of Mrs. Richardson's house and also round the mortuary in old Montague Street, whither the body was quickly conveyed. As the body lies in the rough coffin in which it has been placed in the mortuary—the same coffin in which the unfortunate Mrs. Nicholls was first placed—it presents a fearful sight. The body is that of a woman about 45 years of age. The height is exactly five feet. The complexion is fair, with wavy dark brown hair; the eyes are blue, and two lower teeth have been knocked out. The nose is rather large and prominent.

One of many broadsheets circulating Whitechapel. This one announcing the capture of the mysterious 'Leather Apron' who was subsequently released by the police even though identified by many living at 35 Dorset Street

Elizabeth Stride's boyfriend and murderer, Michael Kidney, a man known for his violent behaviour and temper

A newspaper's view of the interview between Matthew Packer and Inspector Abberline. Most dismiss Packer as a witness but his evidence is crucial to the explanation of Elizabeth Stride's behaviour on the night of her murder

Frances Coles, who many dismiss as a victim of the Ripper. However, something certainly happened after her death and the arrest of Thomas Cutbush which finally made the police close their Ripper files. She also, at one time, was resident at 35 Dorset Street

Thomas Sadler was cleared of the murder of Frances Coles but the Metropolitan Police continued to hound him for months afterwards

choose'. A man in fact who could pull a curtain down on the maniac inside and display to the world this fatherly gentle figure, but when the curtain lifted here was a man whose voices told him to murder hundreds of children. He would then eat them and then send boasting letters to the parents of his victims describing 'how sweet her tender little body was, roasted in the oven. It took me nine days to eat her'.

So it is clear that it would be a great mistake to think of a paranoid schizophrenic as always being the wild, dishevelled killer with blazing eyes that is usually in our imagination. No, sometimes these killers are unusually adept at hiding their demons and voices, like Earle Leonard Nelson who travelled the USA strangling and mutilating women in the 1920s, with his Bible clutched in one hand and a comforting prayer on his lips to disarm his victims. As Ronald Markman, the well-known American forensic psychiatrist and attorney, remarks:[7]

> Psychosis is a medical condition in which the person loses contact with reality in a profound manner. Thoughts, perceptions, feelings, and behaviour become severely disorganized, and the personality begins to deteriorate. The psychotic person displays distorted perceptions, delusion, and hallucinations, and is compelled by these misperceptions to respond to people or situations in a bizzare, disorganized 'crazy' fashion ... Psychosis comes and goes. A person who seems perfectly normal one minute can deteriorate into a psychotic 'episode' within minutes. If he commits a terrible crime during his psychotic episode, he may believe he is actually doing his victim a favour.

Ted Bundy – who was featured in an earlier chapter – was a perfect specimen of the strange beast that typifies the second category: the controlled, calculating murderer. Intelligent, cool, charming and with a smile that could and did disarm a hostile jury trying him for murder. A man who carefully planned his kidnapping of young girls, donning false plaster casts on his arm or using crutches so that the girls helped this handsome smiling young man back to his car, probably hoping for a date with him. But when the handcuffs were snapped on their wrists with astonishing speed and they were brutally shoved into the car, they quickly saw the other side of Bundy. He was cold and calculating with absolutely no feelings for his victims, they were mere objects to serve his purpose. His treatment of the girls he kidnapped, brutally raped and then murdered was horrific. Norman Collins is another extreme example of the controlled killer, to all intents and purposes a normal healthy young man who had no trouble getting regular dates with the girls of Ann Arbor. Seven brutal murders later in 1970, he sat in the court as if carved from stone as the evidence of his appalling crimes was read out. If anyone had dared to suggest to either of these two killers that devils or demons were behind their work they would have been extremely offended. They enjoyed the power of having their victims completely under their control, their sexual slaves to abuse and then snuff out when they had satisfied their lust.

This is the type of killer that Markman calls 'sociopaths'.[8] They do not kill because they feel threatened 'but because they totally lack inner restraints, or conscience, in the first place. Sociopaths kill when the outer restraints – policemen and other restricting circumstances – are missing and the death of the victim means removing an obstacle or enjoying a godlike rush of power over another person'.

The out and out sex maniac is another category. A man who just cannot satisfy his sexual appetite and has to go out and rape … and to avoid capture murders his victims. This is the type of killer who given unlimited freedom to indulge his sexual appetite would probably not kill again. This category of sex criminal is not like the controlled killer at all. Generally he has no charm or manners and carries out his attacks in a brutal haphazard manner. John Duffy, the 'Railway Rapist' of the 1980s in the London area clearly belongs to this group, a brute of a man, skilled in martial arts, a wife beater who picked his victims as opportunity presented them, forced them into brutal sex and only began murdering them when one girl almost identified him. He was simply after sex, the murder was necessary only to avoid capture.

The fourth type is somewhat rarer than the others: the frustrated little man whose ego is not strong enough for him to engage in normal social activity. John Reginald Christie is the classic example, murdering seven women so that he could have sexual relations with them, because he was incapable of doing so while the women were still alive. Joachim Kroll did exactly the same thing in Germany in the 1960s and 1970s, killing his young female victims because he was too shy to attempt sexual contact with a living person.

Of course there are other types of serial killers and of course there are murderers who just can't be categorized. Revenge, jealousy, love and dozens of other human emotions or conditions can all power the motivation to commit murder – even something so simple as 'not liking Mondays' can provide the motive for mass murder as one famous case showed. But it is clear that as the picture of the serial killer has emerged over the last one hundred years, we can see that the killers are, in general, very particular types of animal that *usually* fall into one of the aforementioned categories.

What also emerges is that the killers of category one, the psychotics driven by demons and devils, are *not* sexual murderers in the real sense of the word. They are savage slayers and mutilators, but they do not kill to satisfy their *physical* sexual lust. However the killers of category two, three and four are most certainly sexual murderers, as they intend to have sexual contact with their victims, dead or alive. This is an important distinction to make in the case of the Ripper, because as already mentioned, Jack the Ripper had no sexual contact with his victims. Subsequently, this seems to strongly indicate that he fits into the category of murderers who felt themselves guided and driven by demon voices, the psychotic paranoid schizophrenic. Here lies also the importance of the chapter devoted to the murder and mutilation of Mary Jane Kelly, as often this type of killer is driven by quasi-religious motivations like Earl Leonard Nelson, who was mentioned earlier. He was a serious devotee of the Bible and it would appear from the mutilations carried out on Mary Jane Kelly that Jack the Ripper had also studied his Bible. But perhaps it is still too early to assume that the Ripper belongs to this or that category. However, at least we have another criterion to apply to our suspects, and this is helpful because we can safely assume that Jack the Ripper will fall into one of the categories we have listed above. It will be necessary, to give us firm ground, to repeat the criteria when we come to examine the suspects, but before that it is also necessary to reduce the Ripperologists pack of suspects down to a manageable level.

7 Elimination

You mean, in case it really is two Woozles

The quickest way to dispose of a whole host of Ripperologist suspects is to pose a question. If a newspaper had promoted the theory during the hunt for the 'Yorkshire Ripper' in the late 1970s that the killer could have been a member of the royal family, what would its readers have thought? Let's take it even further than that. What if the same newspaper alleged that the following were also involved with the murder of prostitutes in the north of England: Sir Harold Wilson, the Right Honourable Edward Heath, Mary Whitehouse, Sir Peter Scott, Lord Snowdon and Peter Ustinov.

Make no mistake, the list of suspects from the books concerning Jack the Ripper feature equally prominent public figures from the Victorian age ... and it is the very prominence of the figures that poses a serious question. Why should, or even more importantly how could, such prominent figures suddenly throw aside their public respectability and start murdering and mutilating prostitutes in a red-light district where they would stand out like submarines in the Sahara? The whole idea is so naïve and preposterous that it shouldn't even be entertained, but it has to be – albeit briefly – because the Ripperologists have filled book after book with their extravagant theories and it has stuck in the minds of their readers. Of course these theories involving the highest in the land and murder are enormously popular in much the same way as the marital problems of the royal family are today, but that doesn't mean to say that they are based on any sort of factual evidence. They are theories, speculation of the worst type and are largely backed up by facts that tend to disappear when looked for. We have already seen how these stories can be built up over the years until they assume some kind of reality. Take the case of Mary Jane Kelly again where a whole plethora of stories and theories were built up by the experts based on her pregnancy. At least two books and numerous press articles have taken this single 'fact' and weaved a fairly credible story around it of a 'Jill the Ripper', a murderous midwife who murders and mutilates the women she is supposedly about to abort. But as we have seen Mary Jane Kelly was not pregnant, and this illustrates only too well how these theories spread like an uncontrollable cancer throughout the Ripper world.

It is in much the same way that the Russian secret agents, black magicians, and Irish terrorists all make their appearance in the story of Jack the Ripper. But as we have just seen in the last chapter these people do not really have a place in the gallery of murderers we looked at. For once it is possible to agree with one of Colin Wilson's statements that most modern-day serial killers have working class or lower middle class origins.[1] It must be obvious to one and all that a man intent on committing murder has the cards stacked against him if he is some way famous, in the same way that a high government official who wishes to pick up prostitutes from a well-known red-light district will quickly find himself headline news in the newspapers. On the other hand, a labourer can rest assured that no one is going to make a fuss of his sexual habits, unless he commits murder. And that is the rub. A high public profile generally rules out a person from indulging his vices, particularly when that vice involves something so public as murdering and chopping up prostitutes, and this was as true in 1888 as it is today. No, Jack the Ripper was a very ordinary little man with a very extraordinary bent for murder.

However, the Ripperologists do also have some very plausible suspects and it is to these that we must now turn our attention.

Sir Melville Macnaghten the Chief Constable CID of the Metropolitan Police in 1889, the year after the Ripper murders, is the primary source from which the Ripperologists draw their evidence for the three very strong candidates for Jack the Ripper. This because the chief constable wrote down his thoughts in 1894 on the killings in what has become known as the 'Macnaghten Papers' and to not go too deeply into these papers for the moment, it suffices to say that he maintained that the police suspected three different individuals of being the Ripper. To quote from his original document:[2]

> No one ever saw the Whitechapel Murderer; many homicidal maniacs were suspected, but no shadow of proof could be thrown on any one. I may mention the cases of 3 men, any of whom would have been more likely than Cutbush [Macnaghten wrote the document to exonerate Thomas Cutbush of being the Ripper] to have committed this series of murders:
> (1) A Mr M.J. Druitt, said to be a doctor & of good family, who disappeared at the time of the Millar's Court murder, whose body (which was said to have been upwards of a month in the water) was found in the Thames on 31st Dec – or about 7 weeks after that murder. He was sexually insane and from private info I have little doubt but that his own family believed him to have been the murderer.
> (2) Kosminski, a Polish Jew, & resident in Whitechapel. This man became insane owing to many years indulgence in solitary vices. He had a great hatred of women, specially of the prostitute class, & had strong homicidal tendancies; he was removed to a lunatic asylum about March 1889. There were many circs connected with this man which made him a strong 'suspect'.

> (3) Michael Ostrog, a Russian doctor, and a convict, who was subsequently detained in a lunatic asylum as a homicidal maniac. This man's antecedents were of the worst possible type, and his whereabouts at the time of the murder could never be ascertained.

Sir Robert Anderson, in 1888 the Assistant Commissioner Metropolitan Police CID, also hinted broadly that the Ripper was a Polish Jew and had been confined to a lunatic asylum, and Chief Inspector Swanson, who was directly in charge of the Ripper investigations, also put forward the name of Aaron Kosminski as the chief suspect for the Ripper crimes. So there is a very persuasive case for Aaron Kosminski being the Ripper, after all the testimony of three of the highest police officers in the land all of who were actually involved in the murder investigation cannot be lightly dismissed. Kosminski is an ideal suspect, as he fits in almost perfectly as the missing piece to the Ripper puzzle, a tailor-made suspect who can just about fulfill every criterion we have established in our long quest for the truth. He *was* insane and Dr Houchin who witnessed Kosminski's certification to be confined to the Colney Hatch Lunatic Asylum in February 1891 said of him: 'He declares that he is guided and his movements altogether controlled by an instinct that informs his mind, he says that he knows the movements of all mankind, he refuses food from others because he is told to do so, and he eats out of the gutter for the same reason.'

One wants to leap up and down and shout out 'Jack the Ripper'! Because that is the classic description of a paranoid schizophrenic as we saw in the last chapter. A man like Herb Mullin who was commanded by voices to kill over a dozen people in California in the early 1970s. Voices are telling him what to do and he goes out and does it, here is a man driven by demons and no mistake. But one also has to hesitate, and question. If the three police chiefs were really convinced that Kosminski was their man why did Macnaghten include two other suspects on his list with him? Why did Chief Inspector Swanson in his own documents claim that Kosminski died shortly after being committed to Colney Hatch Lunatic Asylum in 1891 while in fact the man lived on until 1919? And finally, why, if Aaron Kosminski was the Ripper was he allowed to wander at large until February 1891? Remember the police view was that Mary Jane Kelly was the last of the Ripper's victims and her murder took place in November 1888. Macnaghten himself wrote in his document: 'A much more rational theory is that the murderer's brain gave way after his awful glut in Miller's Court [where Mary Jane Kelly was murdered], and that he immediately committed suicide, or, as a possible alternative, was found to be so hopelessly mad by his relations, that he was by them confined in some asylum.'

But we know that to not have been the case with Kosminski, he wasn't committed until over two years later. Macnaghten wrote his memoranda in February 1894, three years after Kosminski had been interred, so if the police were convinced that he was the Ripper why did Macnaghten speculate about Kosminski's fate so long after the event? He must have surely known that Kosminski wasn't committed to a lunatic asylum until two years later – not immediately – and he certainly hadn't committed suicide. This is an obvious reference to Mr M.J. Druitt whose only connection to the entire Ripper fiasco was that he committed suicide by drowning himself in the Thames a few weeks after the murder of Mary Jane Kelly. Apart from that connection – a connection that is so thin that it isn't really a connection at all – there is not a shred of evidence anywhere to link Druitt with the Ripper murders. Although again a host of writers have taken that single point and created books around it.

There is enormous conflict in the separate statements of the three police chiefs. Macnaghten also wrote: 'the Whitechapel murderer, in all probability, put an end to himself soon after the Dorset Street affair in November 1888 ... '

Swanson wrote: 'After the suspect had been identified ... he was watched by police by day and night. In a very short time the suspect with his hands tied behind his back he was sent to Stepney Workhouse and then to Colney Hatch and died shortly afterwards – Kosminski was the suspect ... '

Sir Robert Anderson wrote: 'I will only add that when the individual whom we suspected was caged in an asylum, the only person who had ever had a good view of the murderer at once identified him ... '[3]

One senior policeman believes the murderer to have committed suicide, another claims that the murderer was identified and then confined in the lunatic asylum and the other believes that the murderer was identified actually in the lunatic asylum. Such a conflict amongst three of the senior police chiefs of the time is alarming and points to a very confused situation indeed. And what are we to make of Major Henry Smith's statements – after he had retired as commissioner of the City of London Police – that Sir Robert Anderson's claim to have identified the Ripper was 'irresponsible' and his investigation 'fruitless'?[4]

Major Henry Smith was not the only senior police officer to cast doubts on the statements of his immediate superiors. Inspector Frederick George Abberline, who was one of the most important and knowledgeable police officers connected with all the Ripper murders, gave some interviews to the *Pall Mall Gazette* in 1903 and his statements are persuasive evidence that the top rank of Scotland Yard were being deliberately evasive:

> You can state most emphatically, that Scotland Yard is really no wiser on the subject than it was fifteen years ago. It is simple nonsense to talk of the police having proof that the man is dead. I am, and always have been, in the closest touch with Scotland Yard, and it would have been next to

> impossible for me not to have known about it. Besides, the authorities would have been only too glad to make an end out of such a mystery, if only for their own credit.

At this point the *Pall Mall Gazette* assured its readers that: 'To convince those who have any doubts on the point, Mr Abberline produced recent documentary evidence which put the ignorance of Scotland Yard as to the perpetrator beyond the shadow of doubt.' Then Abberline continued: 'I know ... that it has been stated in certain quarters that "Jack the Ripper" was a man who died in a lunatic asylum a few years ago, but there is nothing at all of a tangible nature to support such a theory.' It is vital to note that Inspector Abberline said this in 1903, that is nine years after Macnaghten and the others made their statements, and as he was probably the most qualified and experienced police officer to investigate the Ripper crimes his opinions must mean that the credibility of the senior police chiefs has to be questioned. Furthermore another Metropolitan Police commissioner, James Monro, still thought the Ripper to be at large as late as September 1889, that being six months after Macnaghten's one suspect Kosminski was removed to an asylum and nine months after his other suspect, Druitt, committed suicide.[5] This just doesn't make any sort of sense. Can it really be possible that five or six of the most senior officers in a single murder inquiry can hold such conflicting opinions when that murder is supposedly solved? Even worse when one of these senior police officers, Inspector Abberline, categorically states that the others are totally wrong in their assumptions? That seems plainly impossible, unless the other officers were deliberately creating this hopelessly confused situation. But why should they do that? Why, indeed.

But for the moment back to the three chief suspects who have up till now been the only really serious candidates for the role of Jack the Ripper. Michael Ostrog is hard to place, he was well known as a confidence trickster and swindler, passing himself off variously as a count, Belgian doctor or Russian surgeon, and he was certainly a dangerous man to cross in the criminal world. But there is no link between him and the Ripper murders and the only reason he was put forward by Macnaghten seems to be that Ostrog was 'available' as a suspect. There is no evidence that Ostrog was in the London area at the times of the Ripper murders. The other two, Druitt and Kosminski, present yet another serious flaw which the Ripperologists have tended to ignore in their search for the Ripper. For if these two men were the chief suspects and the case was considered closed when either Druitt had committed suicide or Kosminski was incarcerated in a lunatic asylum then why did the police search for Jack the Ripper *intensify* after both these occasions?

The Home Office files on the Ripper murders show quite clearly that extra police patrols were drafted into Whitechapel long after Druitt had committed suicide. For instance in January 1889, and again after Kosminski had been locked up in February 1891 the police continued their hunt for the Ripper. A glance at Scotland Yard's own files – specifically on the Ripper murders – shows that they were also not finally closed until 1892.

There can be only one reason why the police continued to investigate these crimes, and why the Home Office sanctioned those investigations, and that must be that the police still believed the Ripper to be at large. What appears to have happened here is that the five senior police chiefs sat down some years after the event and by a process extraordinarily similar to that employed by modern Ripperologists put all the names of the suspects into a big hat and drew out three of the best. Or is there a more sinister design to this totally confusing situation? The answer to this question may lie in Macnaghten's document, not what he said but *why* he said it. The fact of the matter is that the chief constable of Scotland Yard put pen to paper to *defend* the reputation of yet another suspect who had been featured in a series of articles in the *Sun* newspaper in 1894 alleging that he, Thomas Cutbush, was Jack the Ripper. This really quite extraordinary behaviour is without precedent in the case, as many other suspects had been featured in the press – for example John Pizer aka 'Leather Apron' – without Scotland Yard or anybody else leaping to their defence. That Macnaghten rose to the defence of this man and in consequence dragged the other senior Metropolitan police chiefs along with him – except for Major Smith who attacked the claims of these other policemen and most significantly was from the City of London police force – and felt obliged to offer better alternatives to the identity of Jack the Ripper smacks of a conspiracy. Why should a senior police chief feel himself obliged to defend a total stranger who may well have been Jack the Ripper? It is obvious that Macnaghten himself could not have been convinced that any of the three alternatives he put forward as the Ripper were really the murderer. Equally obvious at this stage is the massive conflict of opinion between the Metropolitan and City of London police forces. Even the press were aware of this and lauded the City Police as being frank and helpful with their information about the Ripper murders but claimed the Metropolitan force (Scotland Yard) were obstructive and secretive.

This conflict came to a head at Mary Jane Kelly's inquest when there was an open dispute concerning police jurisdiction and the coroner, Dr Roderick Macdonald, suddenly ended the inquest after cause of death had been established by asking the jury to conclude the proceedings and advised them that: 'There is other evidence which I do not propose to call, for if we at once make public every fact brought forward in connection with this terrible murder, the end of justice might be retarded.'[6] The newspapers and the general public were outraged by Macdonald's behaviour and well they should have been as important witness testimony was not even heard – like that of George Hutchinson who claimed to have had a first-hand view of the murderer of Mary Jane Kelly – and there is absolutely no doubt that Macdonald's strange behaviour did indeed 'retard the end of justice'. The most significant observation that can be made about this particular farce is that the coroner, Macdonald, was employed at the time by the Metropolitan police force as a surgeon. On the other hand the coroner, Wynne Baxter, who conducted most of the other inquests into the Ripper murders was in open conflict with the Metropolitan police force and highly critical of their methods.

One doesn't want to rush headlong on and start screaming about high level Freemason conspiracies involving the highest in the land and various other nonsense as some 'Ripperologists' have done in the past because that is plainly ridiculous. But there is a powerful undercurrent here that demands to be measured, and the best way to do that is to look at the case of Thomas Cutbush and to see if it is possible to find out why Sir Melville Macnaghten, the Chief Constable CID of the Metropolitan Police, was so keen to protect this unknown man.

8 Thomas Cutbush

That buzzing-noise means something. You don't get a buzzing-noise like that, just buzzing and buzzing, without its meaning something. If there's a buzzing-noise, somebody's making a buzzing-noise, and the only reason for making a buzzing-noise that I know of is because you're a bee.

Paul Begg in his otherwise excellent book *Jack the Ripper: The uncensored facts* states: 'Cutbush need not detain us. He was not Jack the Ripper.'[1] So with one line Thomas Cutbush is dismissed from the Jack the Ripper story by – and it must be said because Begg refreshingly sticks to facts – one of the foremost writers on the subject when Cutbush really deserves at least a chapter and to do justice to history we will give him one.

In 1896 an executive superintendent of Scotland Yard sat down in his kitchen and shot himself in the head while his daughter looked on. He had suffered from severe depression for a number of years – he was diagnosed as paranoid and suffering from delusions – and finally committed suicide. His name was Superintendent Charles Henry Cutbush and he was Thomas Cutbush's uncle. It is conceivable that his nephew was partly responsible for Superintendent Cutbush's years of depression and eventual suicide as no senior police officer likes to have a black sheep in the family, particularly when that black sheep is criminally insane and goes around stabbing women with a knife. Thomas Cutbush was twenty-two years old when, in 1888, he suddenly abandoned his work of canvassing the Whitechapel area for a business directory and started to act very strangely indeed, wandering the streets of Whitechapel late at night and returning home in a dirty and muddy condition. Eventually his behaviour became so alarming that he was locked away in Lambeth infirmary as a lunatic on the 5 March 1891 but he managed to escape almost immediately and then subsequently stabbed one woman, Florence Grace Johnson, and attempted to stab another before being arrested on the 9 March 1891. He was judged to be criminally insane and sent off in April to Broadmoor where he died in 1903. Macnaghten throws more light on Thomas Cutbush's history in his 'confidential' memorandum:

> The case referred to in the sensational story told in the 'Sun' in its issue of 13th inst, & following dates is that of Thomas Cutbush who was arraigned at the London County Sessions in April 1891, and on a charge of maliciously wounding Florence Grace Johnson and attempting to wound Isabelle Frazer Anderson in Kennington. He was found to be insane, and sentenced to be detained during Her Majesty's pleasure. This Cutbush, who lived with his mother and aunt at 14 Albert St. Kennington, escaped from the Lambeth Infirmary (after he had been detained there only a few hours as a lunatic) at noon on 5th March 1891 – He was rearrested on 9th idem. A few weeks before this, several cases of stabbing, or 'jobbing' girls behind had recurred in the vicinity, and a man named Colicott was arrested, but subsequently discharged owing to faulty identification. The cuts in the girl's dresses made by Colicott were quite different to the cut made by Cutbush (when he wounded Miss Johnson) who was no doubt influenced by a wild desire or morbid imitation. Cutbush's antecedents were enquired into by Ch. Inspr. (now Supt.) Chis [name illegible], by Inspr. Race and by P.S. McCarthy CID – (the last named officer had

> been specially employed in Whitechapel at the time of the murders there –) and it was ascertained that he was born, & had lived, in Kennington all his life. His father died when he was quite young, and he was always a 'spoilt' child. He had been employed as a clerk and a traveller in the Tea trade at the Minories, & subsequently canvassed for a Directory in the East End, during which time he bore a good character. He apparently contracted syphilis about 1888 and, – since that time – led an idle and useless life. His brain seems to have become affected, and he believed that people were trying to poison him. He wrote to Lord Grimthorpe, and others, – & also to the Treasury. – complaining of Dr Brooks, of Westminster Bridge Rd, whom he threatened to shoot for having supplied him with bad medicine. He is said to have studied medical books by day, & to have rambled about at night, returning frequently with his clothes covered with mud; but little reliance could be placed on the statements made by his mother or aunt, who both appear to have been of a very excitable disposition. It was found impossible to ascertain his movements on the nights of the Whitechapel murders.[2]

That was the man whose name Macnaghten wanted to clear as a suspect in the Ripper murders. Cutbush was quite obviously criminally insane, another classic 'paranoid schizophrenic' suffering typical delusions that people were trying to poison him, writing letters to all and sundry, spending his days reading medical books or alternately drawing pictures of women in indecent postures and threatening to shoot his own doctor … and he liked to stab women. It makes one almost pity Macnaghten's chief suspect Mr M.J. Druitt whose only crime or inclination to crime was to throw himself into the River Thames with a load of stones in his pockets. Macnaghten's memorandum is a monumental disaster of police work and even over a hundred years later it is difficult to believe that a chief constable of Scotland Yard could have expected anyone to accept his utterly fantastic proposal that someone like Druitt was a more likely candidate for the Ripper than Cutbush. It, quite honestly, defies explanation.

Macnaghten goes on to present his evidence as to why Cutbush could not have been the Ripper. Firstly to the knife that Cutbush used to stab the women after his escape from Lambeth Infirmary, Macnaghten ridicules the *Sun* report of the 14 February 1894 which claimed that this knife was the very one used in the Ripper murders. As he quite rightly points out this cannot have been the case as the knife was not purchased by Cutbush until February 1891, two years and three months after the Ripper murders. But that doesn't prove anything apart from the *Sun* was wrong about the knife. Obviously Cutbush would not have been allowed to retain any sort of weapon when he was confined to the Lambeth Infirmary as a lunatic and equally so if he had been in the habit of stabbing women previously he may have lost his knife or simply thrown it away. The evidence of the knife is no evidence at all.

Macnaghten's second point is one that the 'Ripperologists' have clung to with single minded devotion since he wrote it in 1894 and that is: 'It will be noticed that the fury of the mutilations increased in each case, and, seemingly, the appetite only became sharpened by indulgence. It seems, then, highly improbable that the murderer would have suddenly stopped in November '88, and been content to recommence operations by merely prodding a girl behind some 2 years & 4 months afterwards.'[3] Well, on the face of it that seems to be a reasonable point, that a murderer would simply not stop murdering and be content with some lesser criminal activity. But there are comparisons which we can make today which Macnaghten couldn't as he didn't possess the knowledge or information that we now do about such killers, and what these comparisons show is that some killers do indeed vary their behaviour and it cannot be taken for granted that a killer must always go on killing.

In a previous chapter we mentioned several of these

killers but it is worth looking quickly at some of them again to prove the point. The 'Boston Strangler' simply stopped killing women after his thirteenth victim and began to rape them instead, and Colin Pitchfork raped and murdered a Leicestershire girl in 1983 and then was content to expose himself to young women for three years until he murdered again. Often the problem is that we simply do not understand the mechanism that triggers a killer into killing. The case of Colin Pitchfork illustrates this only too well because he admitted he raped and murdered the two girls because they had not acted like the hundreds of other girls he had exposed himself to. The girls were supposed to walk past him and continue on their way but neither did, instead they backed away from him – cutting off his prearranged flight path back to his vehicle. Somehow this behaviour triggered that dangerous 'something' in Pitchfork which resulted in the deaths of the girls. If they had walked past and simply ignored him they would both be alive today. It can be even simpler than that. Kürten the 'Dusseldorf Murderer' was in the habit of walking up to women in broad daylight and demanding sex with them. Surprisingly some agreed, no doubt through fear, and after sex he walked off leaving the women terrified but at least alive. However if a woman said 'no' to him the consequences were truly dreadful, with the woman strangled, battered or stabbed to death within seconds. One servant girl he approached and asked for sex replied, 'I'd rather die!'

'Die, then!' he said and stabbed her. Obviously Kürten's behaviour was much more complex than just that, but it does show that some killers need to be triggered into the act and others *can* simply give up killing.

So Macnaghten's point is not really a valid one, and it is anyway based on the rather shaky premise that the Ripper murders ceased after the death of Mary Jane Kelly in November 1888. But what of the evidence in the last chapter, from the Home Office and Scotland Yard files, that the police were still actively engaged in the hunt for the Ripper for three years after this date, and there *were* a number of unexplained murders of prostitutes in the Whitechapel area *after* November 1888 which some senior police officials and others saw as the work of the Ripper. On 16 July 1889 the body of the prostitute Alice McKenzie was found by a police constable in Castle Alley, Whitechapel. She had been stabbed twice in the throat and her killer had made several mutilations to her torso but had probably been disturbed by the arrival of the constable. Dr Thomas Bond who examined the body said:

> I see in this murder evidence of similar design to the former Whitechapel Murders viz: sudden onslaught on the prostrate woman, the throat skillfully & resolutely cut with subsequent mutilation, each mutilation indicating sexual thoughts & a desire to mutilate the abdomen & sexual organs. I am of the opinion that the murder was performed by the same person who committed the former series of Whitechapel Murders.[4]

The Right Honourable Henry Matthew, Home Secretary at the time, in a comment to the press concerning the murder of Alice McKenzie also confirms that he believed she had been killed by the Ripper. Monro the Metropolitan Police Commissioiner at the time also felt that this was another Ripper murder and moved fifty-six extra police officers into the Whitechapel area to supplement the 102 plain-clothes men he already had patrolling the vicinity, so one is again left in some confusion by the conflicting opinions of the men in charge of the Ripper investigation. An even later murder in February 1891 was also attributed by many of the senior officials involved to the Ripper, that of Frances Coles who was found still alive but with her throat cut and the police constable who found her actually heard a man running away from the scene. Although the police did their utmost to convict a ship's fireman, Thomas Sadler, he was eventually discharged and the verdict given of murder by person or persons unknown. Macnaghten makes it quite clear in his memorandum that he remained convinced that Sadler was the murderer, but he may have held this opinion simply because it suited his own theory that the Ripper murders had ceased in 1888. Equally so it was another line of defence for his favoured Thomas Cutbush, a person who he seems to have decided to protect regardless of the circumstances.

It is useful at this stage to look again at the behaviour of some of the more notorious mass murderers of the last hundred years in relationship to Macnaghten's statements about a murderer not simply giving up murder. But this time without the prejudice of assuming that Jack the Ripper stopped killing in 1888 because, as we will see, a one or two year gap between killings is not at all unusual for these types of criminals.

Ludwig Tessnow brutally mutilated, murdered and dismembered two young girls in Southern Germany in 1897 and it wasn't until 1900 that he did the same to two young boys. In between he had satisfied his desire to mutilate and kill by hacking sheep to pieces. Australian serial killer, Arnold Sodeman, who escaped detection for many years because of his outward 'respectability', murdered a girl in 1930, another one in 1931 and then let five years slip by before he finally murdered June Rushmer and was caught. The 'Southside Slayer', Timothy Spencer, murdered Carol Hamm in Arlington, Virginia, in January 1984 and then remained dormant for three years until he suddenly went on a spree of murder and mutilation that accounted for four more women. The series of murders that took place around the Italian city of Florence which still remain unsolved show a killer with no predictable pattern of behaviour or timing except that he or she likes to kill at a full moon. It is interesting to note that this too is a killer with a bent to mutilate the sexual parts of women. Deaths have occurred on August 1968, September 1974, June 1981, October 1981, June 1982,

September 1983, July 1984 and September 1985. Richard Francis Cottingham declared war on the prostitutes of New York and New Jersey between 1977 and 1980 and murdered and mutilated women in his various hotel rooms but it is important to note that there was a two-year gap between his first and second killing.

These few examples show that one must be extremely careful when trying to explain the behaviour of men who murder. It is plainly not good enough for modern criminologists to support a theory as outdated as Macnaghten's – as many of them do – and perhaps it would be better to say once again that we still simply do not understand the mechanisms that provoke a murderer to murder. As we have seen a killer can go out and commit brutal murder, with just as much savagery as Jack the Ripper, and then slide back into his normal role for as long as three years, before whatever it is that provokes him to murder occurs again. In fact a killer can stop killing – the Boston Strangler demonstrates that as does Colin Pitchfork. The second girl that Pitchfork murdered made the mistake of backing away from him, shutting off his all important escape route. If she hadn't done this he would not have murdered her. He only murdered when the circumstances that he had carefully created to simply expose himself were altered by the victim's unusual behaviour. Pitchfork himself admitted this to the police when he told them that he had exposed himself to more than a thousand females but only felt obliged to murder two of them because they 'provoked' him – rather than motivated him – to attack. In his own words concerning the first murder:

> This is the thing I don't understand about flashing. One per cent of the time you get someone who goes mad and screams and you have to disappear quick. But all the others walk by you. Just walk by you and ignore you. But she turned and ran into a dark footpath. She backed herself

> into a corner ... if she'd walked by, the situation would've disappeared.

And on the second murder:

> I tried to get ahead. I tried to get set, but she was on top of me. I didn't even have time to open me bloody trousers. There's rules to how I play that game. I prefer to do it in a way that satisfies me ... They always have room. No matter where I was exposing meself. No matter where. They always have room to walk by me. It's the easiest way. You shock them. They walk by you and then you got your exit route clear, and go where they come from ...

This second girl also backed herself into a corner, just like the first and died. Pitchfork's thinking is horribly simple: 'It's my game. Play it my way and you live. Break the rules you die.' The problem was that the two young girls didn't know what game they were playing and didn't understand the warped rules. There could be an important lesson for police and parents in Pitchfork's confession. After all, if the girls of the area had been advised by their parents and the police to simply walk past and ignore a 'flashing' man the tragic deaths may not have occurred.

Obviously we are talking about two very different killers here, Jack the Ripper and Colin Pitchfork, as can be seen from the chapter where various types of serial killers were profiled. Pitchfork clearly belongs to the 'Duffy' type who seeks sexual thrill and kills to avoid recognition. But Pitchfork can teach us much about the Ripper – and Cutbush – for he is also a classic example of a killer who *can* give up killing and goes back to committing lesser criminal acts like exposing himself. Pitchfork admitted that for eight months after the first murder he committed no offences whatsoever but then started exposing himself again for a further two years and four months before murdering again. This clearly doesn't fit into any acceptable pattern that has been established by criminologists and psychologists governing the behaviour of killers, but it does clearly demonstrate that Macnaghten's statement – that 'It seems, then, highly improbable that the murderer would have suddenly stopped in November '88, and been content to recommence operations by merely prodding a girl behind some 2 years and 4 months afterwards' – is patently wrong. One cannot rule out a pattern of behaviour on the part of a serial killer where he commits murder and then later reduces his violence to some lesser offence – like exposing himself, killing sheep or stabbing women in the buttocks with a knife.

It is interesting to note that the interval of time given by Macnaghten between 'his' last Ripper killing and Cutbush's reappearance on the streets of London with a knife and Colin Pitchfork's self admitted gap between murders is exactly the same in both cases: two years and four months.

Why was it so vitally important for Macnaghten to continually defend Cutbush against the accusations that he might have been the Ripper? One would have thought under the circumstances that the police would have been more than happy to have had such a prime suspect thrown at them. In more modern times we sadly often see the opposite side of the police coin where suspects are 'fitted-up' by the police to achieve some sort of 'killing rate' but it is not often that we hear or see a chief constable standing up to defend the reputation of a complete and utter criminal maniac like Thomas Cutbush. In fact Macnaghten's defence of Cutbush is probably unique in police history.

Macnaghten was obviously defending his own police department and not just Thomas Cutbush. It was already bad enough that a close relative of a very senior police officer was patently guilty of attacking women with a knife, but the slightest hint that Cutbush could have been Jack the Ripper may well have brought Scotland Yard crashing down to the ground. Especially if it had come out as well that Executive Superintendent Charles Henry Cutbush of Scotland Yard was himself bordering on the verges of lunacy. The newspapers would have had a field day. Don't forget the radical press of the day turned the Ripper murders into a carnival spectacular where the police were mercilessly mocked and ridiculed day after day for their miserable failure to catch the murderer. It was not just the radical press either, the heavy weight conservative papers also joined the campaign, and almost daily during the 1888 murders there were headlines screaming for the resignation of Sir Charles Warren, the Metropolitan Police Commissioner. At mass meetings all over London crowds gathered to hear speeches highly critical of the police and their methods. Sir Charles Warren and the Home Secretary Henry Matthews were singled out when resolutions were passed saying: 'It is high time both men should resign and make way for some other officers who would leave no stone unturned for the purpose of bringing the murderer to justice …[5]

This unprecedented public criticism of the authorities must have pushed a few alarm bells in Scotland Yard and government, and when the press followed it up with scathing comments like this one from the Press Agency then for sure it seemed someone's head had to roll: 'With each fresh murder in the Whitechapel series public alarm has been accentuated and unless something can be done to restore confidence in the detective powers of the police panic will be the result.' Sir Charles Warren was pushed into a very tight corner and when he ultimately did resign on the very day that Mary Jane Kelly was murdered the press was jubilant with headlines like: 'Whitechapel has avenged us!'

If the press could have got hold of a connection between the Metropolitan police force and the murderer – no matter how small – all hell would have broken loose and the confidence of the public in the still fledgling police force would have been well and truly shattered. There is no doubt that the press would have been running headlines the very next day screaming out about a police conspiracy or cover-up. Hot waters indeed and perhaps this is what James Monro, Metropolitan Police Commissioner meant when he later told one of his grandsons that the solution to the Ripper case was a 'hot potato'. A 'hot potato' is no exaggeration and this must be the reason that Macnaghten had for defending Cutbush. The deletion of, or perhaps the deliberate erasion in his memorandum of the name of one of the senior police officers that Macnaghten asked to look into the Cutbush story is also suspicious. The document reads in this section: 'Cutbush's antecedents were enquired into by Ch. Inspr. (now Supt.) Chis ... ' Perhaps Chief Inspector (now Superintendent) Charles Cutbush? That we will never know, but it would have been the sensible and logical thing for Macnaghten to do, to ask the uncle of Cutbush for information about his nephew and this he must have done. Even more confusing, and also highly suspicious, is Macnaghten's single reference in his memorandum to Executive Superintendent Cutbush of Scotland Yard where he refers to him as 'the late Supt. Executive'. Macnaghten signed his memorandum on the 23 February 1894 which is strange as Superintendent Cutbush did not shoot himself until 1896. Of course Macnaghten may have meant 'late' of his department and that Superintendent Cutbush may have taken early retirement, perhaps due to his paranoid delusions? The significance of this will be seen a little later.

And what of the other officers involved in pursuing information about Thomas Cutbush? Inspector William Race actually arrested Cutbush and up till then had been seen as a first-class detective with scores of good arrests to his name. However after the Cutbush affair his career took a sudden downward turn, his expected promotion to superintendent was blocked by his superiors for no apparent cause and instead he was downgraded – because of ill health and depression about his treatment during the Cutbush affair – to be eventually thrown out of the force with a reduced pension. Police constable John McCarthy, the other policeman involved in the Cutbush case, seemed to have fared somewhat better, being promoted to sergeant in the same year that Macnaghten wrote his memorandum about Cutbush. Oddly enough he was transferred at some time, again the record of the date of this transfer in the Scotland Yard files has become 'illegible'. MaCarthy's rise after being made a sergeant was truly meteoric, four years later he was an inspector, six years later a chief inspector and another six years later a superintendent – probably the fastest piece of police promotion in history. Curious isn't it that of the three police officers involved in the Cutbush case two should suffer severe bouts of depression leading in one case to suicide and in the other to enforced early retirement while the other one should go on to become some sort of supercop?

Also somewhat suspicious is the fact that the Home Office and Scotland Yard files covering the period of Cutbush's arrest and the subsequent investigation by the three officers are *missing*. Coincidence or conspiracy of silence. Again it rests on Macnaghten's defence of Thomas Cutbush. Thomas Cutbush very evidently did not deserve Macnaghten's unswerving support. The man was a maniac who liked cutting women with a knife, he was sentenced by a court of law for being a maniac who liked cutting women with a knife and he went to Broadmoor for the rest of his natural life *because* he was a maniac who liked cutting women with a knife. But that still doesn't prove he was Jack the Ripper.

One curious episode in the story of Jack the Ripper came to light when the grandson of Chief Inspector Donald Swanson – who was directly in charge of the Ripper investigation – published notations his grandfather had made in a copy of Sir Robert Anderson's memoirs, *The Lighter Side of My Official Life*. Amongst the several comments made on the Ripper case by Swanson is:

> After the suspect had been identified at the Seaside Home where he had been sent by us with difficulty in order to subject him to identification and he knew he was identified ... On suspect's return to his brother's house in Whitechapel he was watched by police (City CID) by day and night. In a very short time the suspect with his hands tied behind his back he was sent to Stepney Workhouse and then to Colney Hatch and died shortly afterwards – Kosminski was the suspect – D.S.S.

This comment has promoted much confusion amongst the 'Ripperologists' ever since, and not without good reason. For the 'Seaside Home' that Swanson refers to was in fact the 'Convalescent Police Seaside Home' located at West Brighton and opened in March 1890. The question naturally is what the devil were the police up to in sending a homicidal maniac who they themselves were convinced was Jack the Ripper to a police convalescent home by the seaside seventy miles away from London? It surely would have been a simple matter to have had the man identified in London. Why drag him and the witness all the way down to Brighton? But was it, as Swanson claims, Aaron Kosminski that was hauled off to Brighton to be identified? Swanson is obviously mistaken when he says that the suspect, Kosminski, died shortly after admission to Colney Hatch as we know that Kosminski was still alive when Swanson actually wrote his comments in Anderson's memoirs in 1910 and didn't die until 1919. That Swanson cannot really have considered Kosminski to be the Ripper is obvious from one of his private papers where he was added the name of Frances Coles to his list of Ripper victims – she was murdered after Kosminski was under lock and key. If it was really Kosminski why was it necessary to take him and the witness to Brighton? But what if it wasn't Kosminski? What if it was someone else?

Sir Robert Anderson doesn't give much away in his memoirs about the Jack the Ripper case but there are a few statements that make one pause for thought. For example:

> Scotland Yard can boast that not even the subordinate officers of the department will tell tales out of school, and it would ill become me to violate the unwritten rule of the service … I am almost tempted to disclose the identity of the murderer … But no public benefit would result from such a course, and the traditions of my old department would suffer.[6]

What was Anderson trying to say here? For if the suspect had been identified as Kosminski and if the Metropolitan police knew that Kosminski was Jack the Ripper what possible harm could it have done for anybody to say so? Why would Anderson's old department suffer if he disclosed the identity of Jack the Ripper? And Anderson's somewhat sly reference to telling tales out of school could be plainly interpreted as 'the police looking after their own'. Yet again a case of deliberate confusion but this time with a nasty edge of smugness to it.

To try and clear up this mess we can take a closer look at some of the facts we have already taken into account but this time push them into a direction which might help to clear the air.

1 Thomas Cutbush was first confined to the Lambeth Infirmary on 5 March 1891. This means his behaviour sometime in February must have become so alarming that he had come to the attention of the police who eventually had him committed because he represented a danger to the general public.

2 Frances Coles was murdered in Whitechapel on 14 February 1891.

3 The Home Office started to shut down their file on Jack the Ripper in March 1891, the last entry being a request for

extra payments to be met for police patrols in the Whitechapel area.

4 Scotland Yard started to run down their investigation in February/March 1891 as their files show. The only continued interest was in trying to vainly prove that Thomas Sadler had murdered the prostitute Frances Coles.

However one looks at it, the facts are inescapable. There is a solid link between Thomas Cutbush and the coincidental events that took place in February and March of 1891. Remember Aaron Kosminski was already locked up by 4 February 1891 so he couldn't possibly have murdered Frances Coles on 14 February. This event – when they must have thought they finally had the Ripper, or at least a good 'fit-up' for him, under lock and key – must have thrown the entire metropolitan force into total panic which was why it was so important to them to prove that Thomas Sadler had murdered Frances Coles. Anybody but Jack the Ripper. The inquest into Frances Coles' murder was another elaborate farce with the police objecting to a Mr Albert Bachert taking his place as a reserve juror because as a member of the Whitechapel Vigilance Committee – formed during the Ripper murders to prompt the police into action – they knew he would not be satisfied with the police claims that this was not a Ripper murder. The police were determined, hell or high water, to bury Jack the Ripper even if it meant sticking their own heads in the sand so that they couldn't see him anymore.

They were prepared to have anyone as the killer as long as it wasn't Thomas Cutbush. The Scotland Yard files make it plain that the Metropolitan Police force was determined to get Sadler for the murder even if it meant chasing him to the grave. Over a year after Sadler had been proved innocent of the crime Scotland Yard were still recording his daily movements in the hope of nailing him for something. But Thomas Cutbush was allowed to slip into the obscurity of an early death in the securest prison in the land. Macnaghten said that Cutbush was 'found to be insane, and sentenced to be detained during Her Majesty's pleasure' after he had stabbed just one woman with a knife in the bottom. Make no mistake, what Macnaghten meant is that Cutbush was sentenced to be confined for the rest of his natural life if it was Her Majesty's pleasure. John Pizer, another Ripper suspect received six months for stabbing someone in the hand. Charles Ludwig, yet another Ripper suspect, attempted to stab a prostitute and later attacked a man at a coffee stall with a knife and was remanded in custody for a week. Both of these suspects were known by the police to be insane.

It seems rather harsh that if all Thomas Cutbush really did was to stab a woman in the bottom that he was sentenced to be confined to Broadmoor for the rest of his natural life. No, the police must have known a hell of a lot more about the dangerous activities of Cutbush for such a sentence to have been passed. After all the state punishment for a criminal who had murdered but was found to be insane was to be detained at Her Majesty's pleasure.

But back to the 'Convalescent Police Seaside Home' at Brighton. It might seem somewhat superfluous to say that a police convalescent home is there for policemen to convalesce, but given the sort of disinformation we have been forced to swallow from some very intelligent high ranking police officers perhaps it is not out of place. We have already seen that Cutbush's uncle, executive Inspector Cutbush, was a seriously ill man, suffering from depression and paranoia, and it can't have made him leap about with joy when his nephew was apprehended running round Whitechapel, covered in mud, trying to stab women. It seems eminently more logical to believe that either the strange reference to the police seaside home occurs because the man capable of identifying Jack the Ripper was actually at the seaside home because of his ill health, and that means he must have been a policeman. There is no disputing the fact that Inspector Cutbush was in desperate need of a spell in a convalescent home. Or equally that the Ripper suspect in company with a police officer was sent down from London to spend some time away from London where his identity might become known to the press, and this would only have been necessary if the suspect was a policeman or a near relative of one.

Whatever the case, it is obvious that this suspect could not have been Kosminski as the various police chiefs have claimed. Kosminski was already confined when Frances Coles was murdered on 14 February 1891 and there is now absolutely no doubt that something had occurred *after* this murder in late February or early March that made Scotland Yard and the Home Office decide to close their files on the Ripper murders. The only thing that happened in the entire Ripper case after the murder of Frances Coles was that Thomas Cutbush was taken into custody and eventually placed in the Lambeth Infirmary on 5 March from where he quickly escaped and started stabbing women until being re-arrested on 9 March. And after that he was sentenced in April to be detained at Her Majesty's pleasure in Broadmoor ... and Jack the Ripper simply walked out of history and died.

For those who are not prepared to believe that a police force is capable of wholesale deceit – even in cases where extremely violent criminal acts are concerned – when it comes to protecting one of their own, a case which came to light in Germany in 1991 will serve as a convincing example. The modern German case is also a striking illustration of how a criminal with a relation highly placed in the police force that is seeking him can avoid capture and continue his crimes.

A series of particularly brutal rapes took place in and around the university grounds of Essen in the Rhine-Ruhr area. The student victims described the same attacker in each case to the local police and there was a massive hunt for the rapist who police feared would soon turn to murdering his victims because of his callous and violent brutality. The Essen police staked out areas where they knew the rapist operated, they had police officers as decoys and used just about every method of detection available to a modern police force to catch their man. But the rapist was clever, so damned clever that he seemed to know on any given night exactly where the police would be operating and took himself off to another area of the university and raped a victim there. No matter how often the police changed their tactics the rapist moved exactly with them and they eventually came to the reluctant conclusion that the rapist must be one of them, and began to investigate their own officers involved in the case.

Unbeknown to the Essen police, in the nearby town of Bochum a girl had gone to the local police and informed them that she and several of her friends believed her ex-boyfriend to be the rapist as he fitted the police identikit picture perfectly and was well known for his brutal, strange and perverse behaviour. Far from welcoming the co-operation of the girl the police dismissed her out of hand and she was then subjected to a long and fairly dirty campaign by various police officers to make her withdraw her accusations against the man she had implicated. She was also the subject of various threats from the police which eventually made her move out of the area. It was only quite by chance, months later, when she was telling her story to a group of friends in a bar that an off-duty police detective heard it and asked her to repeat it in front of his senior officer. They contacted the Essen police who were appalled by what they heard because the rapist had continued to attack students long after the girl had gone to the Bochum police, but they were even more appalled when they found out that the man implicated by the girl was the son of a very senior police officer in the Bochum police force.

When the Essen police tried to investigate the circumstances of the girl's claims they were met by open hostility from the Bochum police but eventually they won through and consequently found overwhelming evidence that the local police had interfered with witness statements, lost files intentionally and had indeed been harassing the girl because of her accusations against the son of one of their fellow officers.

Until the very last the Bochum police proclaimed the innocence of their colleague's son but he was arrested by the hard-headed Essen police officers and charged with the multiple rapes. It transpired later that the boy's father, the very senior police officer, had been quite happily feeding his son day-to-day information about the activities of the Essen police trying to trap the rapist enabling him to go out and attack a girl somewhere else that night. He had even done this after his son had been accused of the rapes.

History doesn't seem to change much when it comes to the world of crime or police cover-ups. The same sad elements are there in the Essen case of 1991 and in the Thomas Cutbush case of 1881. One hundred years later and nobody seems to have learnt from experience, least of all the police. Of course the Jack the Ripper case was political dynamite in comparison to the Essen/Bochum case where if the police had faced the facts it would have probably meant the early retirement of one of their senior officers, though one can't help wondering how much confidence the people of Bochum now have for their local police after that disgusting fiasco. But the parallels between the two cases are still there: Missing files, illegible or tampered evidence and the almost unbelievable defence of a criminal maniac by senior police officers because that criminal maniac was related to a senior police officer.

Throughout the entire period of the Ripper crimes, there is an underlying current of constant police disinformation and deliberate suppression of facts and evidence, particularly whenever that evidence concerned the possible identity of the Ripper. During the inquest into the circumstances of Catherine Eddowes murder – she was found murdered and mutilated in Mitre Square, Whitechapel on 30 September 1888 – the solicitor acting for the Metropolitan Police, Mr Crawford, stopped Joseph Lawende as he was about to describe her killer to the inquest by saying: 'Unless the jury particularly wish it, I have a special reason for not giving details as to the appearance of this man.'[7]

Therefore Joseph Lawende, perhaps the only man to have ever had a good view of the Ripper, was not permitted to describe the killer's appearance to a court of law. This was obviously to prevent the press from publishing a description of the Ripper. But since when did it ever hurt a murder enquiry to publish the description of the murderer? The press latched onto this immediately. The *Yorkshire Post* reporting that: 'The police apparently have strict orders to close all channels of information to members of the press.' The *Evening News* claiming that: 'The police are extraordinarily reticent with reference to the Mitre Square tragedy.' Across the Atlantic Ocean even the *New York Times* felt that the police: ' ... devote their entire energies to preventing the press from getting at the facts.'

All in all a rather perverse situation with the police working hard to suppress information that may have eventually led to the identification of the murderer and seemingly determined to keep something of vital importance covered up. Whatever that 'something' was never became known but newspaper accounts of the time make it plain that Joseph Lawende was the key to it. He was guarded by two detectives, the police were paying all his expenses and had also imposed a pledge of secrecy on him.

Could it be that Lawende's eyewitness testimony may

have harmed the 'traditions' of Sir Robert Anderson's and Macnaghten's old department who 'never told tales out of school'?

9 Thomas: A Lonely Boy?

What do I look like?
You look like a Bear holding on to a balloon.

Although the evidence connecting Thomas Cutbush with the crimes of Jack the Ripper appears to be largely circumstantial, it is as well not to forget many of the murder cases that were examined earlier where the police failed to act on the alarming coincidences that occurred. In particular the 'Yorkshire Ripper' and 'Ted' murders should be borne in mind, where there were so many circumstantial factors indicating that both Peter Sutcliffe and Ted Bundy were indeed the killers but the police still failed to make the obvious and vital connections. The alarming coincidences that occur in Cutbush's case are further compounded by what is an obvious police effort to disarm a potentially explosive situation, and considering this it is no wonder that Scotland Yard and Home Office files are missing and others have been tampered with. As we have seen the disinformation campaign waged by Scotland Yard on behalf of Thomas Cutbush over a hundred years ago is still to this very day extremely difficult to penetrate. It's as if every time we get a momentary glimpse into the life of this strange man a heavy curtain falls down and blocks everything out. That one of the most factual and accomplished writers on the subject of Jack the Ripper, Paul Begg, can categorically state in 1988 that Thomas Cutbush was not the Ripper when the actual facts seem to indicate otherwise is proof enough of the legacy of falsehood that was established by Macnaghten when he rose to champion the cause of Thomas Cutbush in 1894.

The spectacular defence of Cutbush by a chief constable of Scotland Yard must be a landmark in the history of the British police force, but at the same time it is also very persuasive evidence that something was being hushed up. After all if one has an itch one scratches it and when the *Sun* newspaper claimed in 1894 that Cutbush was Jack the Ripper, Scotland Yard began to scratch as if they had been invaded by a horde of bed bugs.

One wonders what the modern-day Bochum police force would have done with their own violent criminal, the son of one of their senior officers, if the Essen police had simply accepted their assurances that the man was innocent and dropped the case? It is tempting to think that the violent rapist would have been rapidly consigned to a mental institution and his father forced into early retirement, thereby avoiding the painful publicity that the arrest for the crimes would have caused. Perhaps a few years later the father of the rapist, appalled at his own complicity in the horrifying crimes and with his professional career in tatters, might sit down in his kitchen and commit suicide by shooting himself in the head with a pistol? And perhaps one hundred years later, legions of writers would be exercising their imaginations in trying to determine who really was the 'Essen University Rapist'.

Of course, it is only speculation, but the series of events connected with Thomas Cutbush, his uncle Superintendent Cutbush, Jack the Ripper and Scotland Yard provide this exact scenario, and this is probably what happened one hundred years ago when Thomas Cutbush was consigned to Broadmoor for the rest of his natural life.

Sadly, hard facts about the life of Thomas Cutbush are rare things to find. Macnaghten's memorandum leaves much unsaid but it does give us a momentary glimpse into the life of this strange young man and some clues to his behaviour and background. Macnaghten says that Cutbush was 'employed as a clerk and traveller in the Tea trade at the Minories, & subsequently canvassed for a Directory in the East End ... ' This was up till 1888 when Cutbush 'contracted syphilis ... led an idle and useless life. His brain seems to have become affected ... ' This puts Thomas Cutbush right into the centre of Jack the Ripper's territory in 1888, for the Minories is located directly off Aldgate High Street and Whitechapel High Street within a stone's throw of Mitre Square, the murder site of Catherine Eddowes. As a clerk and traveller in the tea trade Cutbush would have had a superior knowledge of Whitechapel, especially when he later went on to canvass for a business directory of the East End. His knowledge of commercial sites in the Whitechapel area would have been considerable, especially when those commercial sites involved the tea trade.

Mary Nichols was murdered on the 31 August 1888 directly outside a tea warehouse.

Catherine Eddowes was murdered on the 30 September 1888 directly outside a tea warehouse.

Annie Chapman was murdered on the 8 September 1888 directly outside a business that built packing cases for the tea trade.

Two later victims were also murdered at commercial premises: Alice McKenzie on the 17 July 1889 at a contractor's yard and Frances Coles on the 13 February 1891 outside a warehouse.

So now we have a man, Thomas Cutbush, known to be a lunatic with a peculiar desire to knife women, who was not only in the Whitechapel area at the time of the Ripper murders but also must have a good working knowledge of at least three of the murder sites if not them all. What else can be learnt from Chief Constable Macnaghten's memorandum? 'He [Cutbush] is said to have studied medical books by day, and to have rambled about at night, returning frequently with his clothes covered in mud ... It was found impossible to ascertain his movements on the nights of the Whitechapel murders.'

If Cutbush rambled about at night and frequently came home with his clothes covered in mud (though two sources print the word 'blood' here in the memorandum rather than 'mud') then why hadn't he come to the attention of the police before 1891? What about in 1888 at the height of the Ripper murders when there were hundreds of policemen swarming the streets of Whitechapel looking for someone just like Cutbush? The mud would have been useful to hide any blood stains. Macnaghten said it was impossible to ascertain Cutbush's movements on the nights of the Whitechapel murders. In other words we are asked to believe that this young lunatic was free to roam the streets of Whitechapel all night long, covered in mud, at the height of the Ripper murders and despite intense police activity was never apprehended?

It is much more likely that he was stopped by the police on numerous occasions but they probably knew him well enough to have escorted him home or to his uncle's house, or to have simply ignored him and said to themselves 'there goes old Superintendent Cutbush's daft nephew again'.

Of course it may have happened like it did in Bochum. With Superintendent Cutbush assuring his fellow police officers that his nephew was a bit simple but harmless enough, and then proceeding to tell his nephew over a cup of tea the latest police tactics to catch the Ripper. Macnaghten's admission that they couldn't trace Cutbush's movements on the all-important nights of the

Ripper murders is a bit mysterious. Why not? Perhaps because Cutbush was not at home on those nights. Perhaps he was taking advantage of his superb knowledge of the area by renting beds in common lodging houses located near commercial sites well known to him and then luring prostitutes into these dark and dismal sites to kill and mutilate them. Perhaps Crossingham's at 35 Dorset Street?

We know that Cutbush was insane and no stranger to either the knife or the immediate area of Jack the Ripper's crimes but what about his motive? It was for this very purpose that all the other killers and their motives were profiled in length in earlier chapters so that at least we would be in a position to profile possible suspects and their motives at this stage. In this way it was possible to say earlier on that Liz Stride's killer was Michael Kidney but it was highly unlikely that he was Jack the Ripper. He just didn't fit the profile of the full-blown psychotic, a paranoid schizophrenic, who hears voices ordering him to kill, voices from demons or God ordering him to kill – but Thomas Cutbush does. Cutbush was without a doubt a full-blown psychotic and it wasn't because he had contracted syphilis in 1888 and his brain had become affected as Macnaghten maintained. We all know now that syphilis has a particularly slow influence on the functions of the body, and if Cutbush had contracted the disease in 1888 it certainly wouldn't have 'affected' his brain in the same year, or for many years later. No, Cutbush's problems were a lot deeper than the onset of venereal disease, though that too may have played a warped role in his later actions.

Thomas Cutbush came from a family with obvious sanity problems. He was insane, his uncle was suffering from 'paranoid delusions' and eventually committed suicide by shooting himself in the head, and his mother and aunt were described by Macnaghten as of 'very excitable disposition' upon who 'little reliance' could be placed. Cutbush's father died while he was very young leaving him in the care of what sounds like his fairly demented aunt and mother, and he was described as 'always being a spoilt child'.

From this short family background it is possible to draw a few conclusions about his character: spoilt, a loner with obvious emotional problems caused by the separation and later death of his father and subsequent upbringing by two excitable women. If he had turned to his uncle in search of a father figure then it probably would not have been a rewarding experience either given that man's own mental instability.

Cutbush's mental state is obvious from Macnaghten's memorandum where the Chief Constable wrote: ' … he [Cutbush] believed that people were trying to poison him. He wrote to Lord Grimthorpe, and others, and also to the Treasury, complaining of Dr Brooks, of Westminster Bridge Rd. whom he threatened to shoot for having supplied him with bad medicines.' This is classic behaviour for a paranoid schizophrenic like Thomas Cutbush, the belief that he is being poisoned and writing letters to all and sundry, regardless of the connection. One could understand Cutbush complaining to a medical council or hospital about his supposed mistreatment at the hands of a doctor but the Treasury or Lord Grimthorpe?

It is well worth looking at another case of Ripper-like crimes as it allows an even better view of the behaviour of Thomas Cutbush.

Edward Gein had a similar upbringing in the USA in the 1900s – his father either dead, or departed for newer pastures, and being dominated by his obsessive mother who religiously rammed down her obviously half-simple son's throat the notion that sex and women in general were sinful things. But when his mother died, simple Ed Gein decided to investigate the things his mother had tried to teach him to despise. He bought serious medical books and spent years studying the female body as portrayed in these type of books which present the human form dissected into its various individual components. From books he moved on to bodies which he dug up out of the local graveyard and kept at his farm, and then he took his macabre interest over the next hurdle and started to kidnap women from the local area. These were brought back to the farm and simple Ed murdered and mutilated them, cutting out their organs to store in his fridge and making souvenirs from other parts of the body. When he was eventually caught it was obvious that Edward Gein did not really know that he had done a terrible wrong and he spent the rest of his life, until 1984, living a model life as a prisoner in various lunatic asylums.

Gein gives us a remarkable insight into the mind of Thomas Cutbush, for the two men not only shared remarkably similar childhoods, they also shared an obsession with reading medical books. Remember what Macnaghten said in his memorandum: 'He [Cutbush] is said to have studied medical books by day ... scribble drawings of women in indecent postures were found torn up in Cutbush's room.'

Pornography would not have been as easily available to Cutbush as it was to Edward Gein some fifty years later and Gein certainly supplemented his collection of medical books with pornography. But the jump from medical books to pornography in both their cases is of great importance and shows what path Cutbush was following. An unhealthy progression from 'allowed' medical pictures of naked women displaying their 'forbidden' internal and external parts to 'forbidden' pornography where the women are 'allowed' to show their 'forbidden' parts. And what comes then? Obviously in Gein's case what came next was a desire to possess those forbidden organs. It seems likely that Cutbush was also obsessed by the same desire to possess these forbidden parts of a female form that he could only fantasize about with the help of his medical books and self-made pornography.

It seems that Edward Gein was incapable of viewing his victims in their totality, rather he saw them as bits and pieces – organs – and there is no evidence that he sexually abused his victims, dead or alive, and this perhaps brings us closer to a fair portrait of Jack the Ripper – or Thomas Cutbush. An important difference must be that Cutbush was suffering from syphilis. This means he had, at some stage, taken his experiments with medical books and pornography further than Edward Gein, but with catastrophic results. Edward Gein was a man who was forced to study medical books to learn about the 'forbidden and sinful' reproductive organs of the female species, as he never had a chance to explore the normal and natural avenues that childhood offers to most of us in this universal quest for the unknown. He was a man who was brought up by a mother who perversely hated her most vital biological function and taught her son that the act of sex, or the essential female partner in sex, is evil and sinful.

This is a vicious dead end of hate that has only one narrow escape channel and that is the murder and mutilation of women. The mother teaches her son that women are sinful, she teaches him that sex is sinful and when he begins to learn – by studying remote medical books – that he has been brought up to hate the very thing that created him then he finds himself in a bitter wilderness that offers no apologies for his very existence. He is damned, along with the rest of the human race and his answer is to attack that which is responsible: the reproductive organs responsible for bringing sin into the world. And if he goes to church or has his Bible there by his side he can find solace for his convictions.

Thomas Cutbush would have been in an even more terrifying predicament than Edward Gein for Cutbush had discovered the awful truth: that the reproductive organs of women were sinful and did bring sin into the world, for after contact with a prostitute he was diseased, unclean, and he would have fully understood the message encoded in Corinthians (6:13–17):

> The body is not meant for sexual immorality, but for the Lord, and the Lord for the body ... Do you not know that your bodies are members of Christ himself? Shall I then take the members of Christ and unite them with a prostitute? Never! Do you not know that he who unites himself with a prostitute is one with her body?

Thomas Cutbush had sinned. He had united the body of Christ with a prostitute and the 'saviour of the world' had contracted syphilis but then he would have known what to do about it: 'Put to death, therefore, whatever belongs to your earthly nature: sexual immorality, impurity, evil desires and greed, which is idolatry.' (Colossians 3:5) This is exactly the type of thinking that went hand in hand with the total religious suffocation and Bible thumping of the Victorian age. It was an age of assertive masculinity where a gang of men could publicly rape and beat a girl while a crowd of unlookers cheered them on, and to viciously assault a girl was considered no more serious than spinning a top on the public highway. This was a very dangerous brew indeed and the only wonder is that there were not hundreds of Jack the Rippers running around London in 1888.

Killers with a mission. Highly dangerous paranoid schizophrenics conditioned by family, church and society to view the female form as a bundle of sinful organs, and with the burning conviction that they were some sort of saviour who has to rid the world of this evil. We are able to see exactly this type of thinking in the behaviour of dozens of later murderers.

But before that let us see what else can be found out about Thomas Cutbush from original sources. The *Sun* newspaper tells a very different story than does Macnaghten in his notes and also provides in its reports of

February 1894 awfully persuasive evidence that Thomas Cutbush was indeed Jack the Ripper.[1]

Thomas Cutbush came from a very unhappy home where his father beat his mother so often that the two were separated while Thomas was still a child. In his younger days he took to wandering the streets of Whitechapel all night long, entering and leaving the house by climbing through the windows. Neighbours often spied him leaping over fences and clambering over walls with the agility of a monkey. During the day he confined himself to his room, hardly ever speaking to his hysterical mother and aunt, and studied medical books. Later this was to be his pattern of behaviour as well, right through the period when the Ripper crimes were committed. Although Cutbush managed to find employment at the time of the Ripper murders it did not last long because he was dismissed rather rapidly. The reason for his dismissal was his strange and sometimes aggressive behaviour. Rather than working he would spend hours looking at himself in the mirror (interestingly this was also one of Peter Sutcliffe's vanities) and when an old man commented on this Thomas Cutbush promptly threw him down a long stairway where he lay concussed and bleeding. Cutbush told the crowd who gathered around the unconscious old man: 'Poor gentleman, he has fallen downstairs.' It was only when the 'poor gentleman' recovered some weeks later that he was able to tell his employers it was in fact Cutbush who had pushed him down the stairs and Cutbush was dismissed.

Fellow workers had often noticed that Cutbush had blood on his sleeves and when detectives investigated his room they found waistcoats and coats that had been hidden, stuffed up the chimney, with suspicious stains which he had attempted to remove with turpentine. They also found various obscene drawings in red ink which he had made, one in particular of a naked woman with her body ripped open and the intestines exposed. Further questioning by the detectives revealed that Cutbush had once attacked a servant girl and on another occasion had grabbed his aunt and tried to slit her throat with a knife.

From Macnaghten's statements concerning Cutbush one gets the impression that he was a weak, sickly individual but that this is far from the truth is born out by his escape from Lambeth Infirmary on 5 March. In the infirmary he was stripped of all his clothes and guarded by four male attendants, notwithstanding such severe security (which also makes one wonder what it was all about if Cutbush wasn't really a dangerous individual) he sprang from the bed, knocked all four men down and disappeared out of a supposedly escape-proof room in a matter of seconds. Still stark naked he scrambled over the infirmary wall and raced through back gardens using his surprising agility to scale walls and fences, dashed into the back door of a house and re-emerged on the street, fully clothed in a matter of minutes to join in the hue and cry for the naked lunatic that had just escaped from the infirmary.

Now we are beginning to see a very different type of Thomas Cutbush than Macnaghten and others would have us believe in. Not only was he psychotic, he was also a powerful, dangerous and agile man capable of unbelievable violence. After all it is not everybody who could knock out four guards and make good their escape from a secure mental institution while stark naked. Hardly the physical behaviour of a man in the last stages of syphilis as Macnaghten would have us believe.

Finally when Cutbush came to court for the stabbings on the two ladies (where he had stabbed them in the bottom) both counsel for the defence and prosecution stated their belief that Cutbush was Jack the Ripper, but they were ignored and Thomas Cutbush was not allowed to plead.

Yes, the *Sun* certainly tells a different story to Scotland Yard and one is left with the feeling that a major newspaper of the day would not have devoted page after page of copy (the extensive reports appeared on 13, 14, 15, 16, 17, 18 and 19 February), six years after the Ripper crimes had been committed, without good reason.

A much later case involving a similarly disturbed young man will illustrate exactly what sort of person Thomas Cutbush really was.[2] Richard Chase was born into a home where there was a good deal of friction between his mother and father, eventually leading to a separation in 1972 when he was twenty-two years old, and he too was a child fond of locking himself up in his room all day then wandering the deserted streets of Sacramento at night. After his parents split up he divided his time between them and his behaviour became even stranger, lying in bed for hours in a trance-like state and then exploding into sudden violent acts like smashing his mother over the head with a telephone. He complained of imaginary illnesses, his head was swelling and the bones were breaking through. Voices began to tell him what to do but he resisted them. His mother heard him telling himself 'I'm not going to do that!' When he went to stay with his grandmother in Los Angeles in 1973 he wandered aimlessly about the house asking himself: 'Are you a good boy?'

'Yes,' he would reassure himself. 'You're a good boy.'

After his grandmother sent him home his father took him to a psychiatrist who reported: 'He has a psychiatric disturbance of major proportions.'

Richard Chase had obviously been studying his medical books as the doctors who examined him reported that he had a good understanding of medical terms. But then he disappointed them by explaining that someone had stolen his pulmonary artery and his blood had stopped flowing. He was further diagnosed as a 'chronic paranoid schizophrenic'. When his mother turned up to collect Richard – against the doctor's advice – they described her as 'highly aggressive, hostile and provocative'. The schizophrenic son had a schizophrenic mother. Back at home by 1976 Richard was sleeping with oranges by his head so that his brain could absorb the vitamin C while he slept. Then he started beating his mother again and was moved out to a small apartment by his father. It was here that he started to drink blood obtained from live rabbits he bought in the neighbourhood; when that didn't satisfy him he began injecting himself with rabbit blood and became violently ill. 'Bad rabbit,' he explained to his father.

Once again taken to hospital he admitted drinking blood to prevent 'his body falling apart' and the doctors diagnosed him this time as 'acute paranoid schizophrenic'. In other words his schizophrenia was blowing up, reaching full strength and he imagined that someone was poisoning him. Richard escaped from the hospital but was brought back again and his condition ranged from long catatonic periods to noisy bouts of disruptive aggression. After a year of heavy medication he was judged fit to be released to his parents. This was a terrible error by the hospital staff for they had just launched on the unsuspecting public a terrible killer who was later to be known as the 'Vampire of Sacramento'. Back at home he became obsessed by the idea that someone was poisoning him, his mind was controlled by others and his organs kept moving around his body. The only way to cure all these ills was to shoot and kill animals in the area and drink their blood and eat their organs. He took to roaming the streets at night in his quest for other people's pets and took them home to kill them. At this time he also started collecting newspaper articles about vicious killings, got hold of a gun and started taking shots at people out of his car, killing one man on his lawn. He was found by several people sitting in their houses or gardens and when chased off disappeared at alarming speed, springing through windows and scaling fences and walls with great agility.

What happened next was so obvious that it should

never have been allowed to happen – but Richard the 'dangerous acute paranoid schizophrenic' had been protected by his schizophrenic mother even after killing her cat in front of her and drinking its blood. He brutally murdered and mutilated a woman after breaking into her house. The crime was a carbon copy of the Jack the Ripper murders, even down to the removal of the same internal organs. Four more people were to die in the same horrifying circumstances before the police caught up with Richard Chase. When they went through his notebooks they found crude drawings of internal organs and newspaper cuttings of various terrible crimes including his own. Once in custody his hallucinations only deepened and he was convinced that he had been given venereal disease by the police and that officers were poisoning his food. It is a sad case which could have been prevented but the parallels that it offers to the case of Thomas Cutbush are astonishing. The broken home, the 'hysterical' or schizophrenic mother, the conviction that they are being poisoned and have venereal disease, the study of medical textbooks, locking themselves in their rooms all day and wandering the streets at night, the peculiar agility and speed in making good their escape, the crude drawings, aggression directed against female relatives and finally the funny speech mannerisms. One can imagine Thomas Cutbush asking himself, 'Are you a good boy?' and one can imagine Richard Chase throwing someone down the stairs and explaining 'Poor gentleman he has fallen down the stairs.'

The evolution of Richard Chase's madness gives us another uncanny view into the mind of Thomas Cutbush, particularly since they were the same age when their 'problems' began. Furthermore it is interesting to note that when the *Sun* reporters went to interview Thomas Cutbush in Broadmoor in 1894 they found a walking zombie, a man in a totally catatonic state, incapable or unwilling of speech and unaware of his surroundings.

This is the typical reaction of a chronic paranoid schizophrenic who has gone through the acute state of explosive, violent behaviour and settled down to spend the rest of his life locked within himself. Sadly we are unable to learn from Cutbush's youth what role religion may have played in his upbringing and illness. However, all the signs would seem to indicate that he too was the victim of a domineering hysterical mother who harboured extreme feelings of hate towards the subject of sex and the female body.

Let us look at the behaviour of some other mass killers – particularly the killers with a mission – since the days of Thomas Cutbush and Jack the Ripper.

Harvey Carignan assured the policemen who arrested him in 1974 for multiple rape, mutilation and murder that they had made a mistake because the person they had arrested – himself – was: 'An Instrument of God, one who was acting under His personal instructions. Murder, rape and mutilation are all part of a Grand Plan. God is a figure with a large hood and you can't see his face.'

A devout and obsessive religious upbringing as a child probably influenced the killer Herbert Mullin to start murdering people in the USA in 1972. Voices told him what to do as he shot four young boys to death in a park at Santa Cruz. When his murder count reached thirteen the police caught him and were no doubt impressed by his claim that he had received telepathic messages from God, and he was in fact the 'saviour of the world' who had saved the world by killing people.

An American civil rights group who attempted to have the sentence of death revoked on the mass-murderer Carl Panzram in 1930 were probably astounded when he told them: 'I wish you all had one neck and I had my hands on it. I believe the only way to reform people is to kill them.' And there it is, said as only someone who has been there and done it could say it: 'To reform people you kill them.' What Panzram was really saying was 'without the shedding of blood there is no forgiveness'. To free people you killed them.

Richard Ramirez is an even better example. When he was handed down nineteen death sentences in Texas in 1985 he informed the court: 'Big deal ... Death comes with the territory ... see you in Disneyland ... Evil, evil ... You maggots make me sick. I will be avenged. Lucifer dwells within all of us.'

The Puerto Rican, Miguel Rivera, kidnapped young boys in the 1970s around Harlem and castrated them because 'God had instructed me to change little boys into little girls'.

The French serial killer, Joseph Vacher, who was examined in an earlier chapter, shouted to the court in 1898 who had sentenced him to death for the murder and mutilation of at least eleven young boys and girls: 'Glory to Jesus! Long live Joan of Arc. Glory to the great martyr of our time! Glory to the great saviour!'

David Berkowitz was born a bastard and dragged through his formative years by a disinterested mother who had him adopted as soon as she could. In 1974 voices started to tell him to kill for his 'Master' and the 'Son of Sam' was born and began to terrorize the city of New York by gunning down innocent people.

An unhappy childhood where his father died when he was five and a later obsession with religion, particularly the idea that atonement could only be obtained from self-inflicted punishment, led Albert Fish to murder and mutilate young boys and girls in the USA in the 1920s and 1930s. When he was led to the electric chair in 1936 he smiled at his captors and told them that he was looking forward to the electric chair as the final experience of true pain. The thinking is totally perverse but had obviously been built up by his religious obsession. Remember the chapter on the death of Mary Jane Kelly? Hebrews 10:22 again: 'In fact, the law requires that nearly everything be cleansed with blood, and without the shedding of blood there is no forgiveness.'

This was Fish's concept. He went out and murdered and mutilated young children, he shed their blood and then he went home and literally whipped himself into a frenzy of remorse and stuck heated needles into his body as punishment. An ever tightening noose of shedding blood followed by forgiveness. If he didn't shed blood then he couldn't be forgiven. He had to atone for his sins, therefore he had to commit them first, and of course the final atonement was his death on the electric chair. But he probably saw himself as a martyr. He had fulfilled his mission, he was free.

When his childhood is examined it is not difficult to see why Fish turned out the way he did. In the Catholic orphanage where he ended up at the age of five he was forced to pray for hours on end every day and was flogged into learning whole chapters of the Bible by heart. The slightest mistake in his Bible learning and the vicious sadist who was supposed to be the matron pulled his pants down and whipped his naked bottom. Fish eventually began to like the flogging and achieved sexual satisfaction from it and throughout his life he associated religion and the Bible with sex and punishment. As he carefully explained to the jury at his trial when asked why he had castrated young boys: 'It is symbolic of Abraham's sacrifice of Isaac.' Feeling that the jury were still not satisfied with his answer he elaborated: 'I am God … my killings were an act of mercy to save the victims from the horrors of life.'

When Jason Nelson – a strict Mormon and seminary student – murdered his baby son as he lay sleeping in the cot in Utah in 1981 by stabbing him with a knife, he was following the instructions of the prophet Abraham which he had received perversely enough while watching 'Mary Poppins' on television.

Another domineering and spiteful mother was probably responsible for the spree of murder that William Heirens embarked on in Chicago in 1945. His mother had literally beaten into him the concept that sex and the female body were evil and dirty things and later in life he was unable to touch a girl without being physically sick. But that didn't stop him murdering and mutilating females. He scrawled on the bedroom wall of one of his victims, 'For heavens sake catch me before I kill more. I cannot control myself.' Interestingly enough he was also a medical student.

Joseph Kallinger was chosen by God to annihilate mankind and funnily enough he interpreted this heavenly message by going out and killing a young boy and then mutilating his body. At his trial in 1976 in New Jersey he claimed to be in daily contact with the Lord and for the benefit of the jury spoke in 'tongues'. His childhood had been appalling with his foster parents teaching him that sex and the sexual organs were evil and wicked and they convinced the impressionable child that he had been castrated to prevent him from contamination with women.

His mother sent Henry Lucas to his very first day at school dressed as a girl and with permed hair. At home he was forced to dress and act like a little girl, when he didn't he was so savagely beaten by his mother that x-rays taken over thirty years later showed that his brain had been severely and permanently damaged. When he eventually broke free from his mother by stabbing her to death when he was twenty-four he was sentenced to forty years in the Ionia State Psychiatric Hospital. Even though he pleaded with the authorities not to free him they let him out early and he went on to kill what is estimated to be two hundred people.

Known as the 'Gorilla Murderer' Earle Nelson murdered and mutilated twenty-two women in a trail of carnage across the USA and Canada in 1926 and 1927. When Nelson was barely a year old his mother died of syphilis which she had caught from his often absent father and the young boy was given into the care of his aunt. She was a religious fanatic who raised her nephew with strict biblical authority and the good book was the be all and end all of their narrow existence. When he was twenty-nine he took his Bible and begun his terrible journey of hate and vengeance across the country, a prayer on his lips for the women he strangled and mutilated. Amazingly at his trial his aunt appeared to vouch for his insanity.

Dayton Rogers was another product of a strict religious upbringing, a Seventh-day Adventist who decided that prostitutes had to pay for the evil in the world and ritualistically murdered seven of them in a peculiar fashion before he was captured in 1987. He had no sexual contact with his victims, satisfying himself by slashing their breasts and ankles with a knife.

A strict religious upbringing led to Thomas Piper taking up the position of sexton at the Warren Avenue Baptist Church but it also led him to murder and mutilate some of his female flock during the 1870s, eventually being caught when he enticed a five year old girl up to the belfry and battered her to death.

The study of medical books in combination with the Bible was certainly a deadly mixture for Sunday School teacher and medical student, Theodore Durrant, as he took to inviting his young female students at the Emanuel Baptist Church into the church library where he left them for a few moments and then reappeared naked. In 1895 he brutally murdered and raped two of them, leaving one victim in the library while he went to preach the word to his Sunday School.

Perhaps the most hideous case on record took place in 1970 on the Canary Islands when the male members of a fanatically religious German family brutally murdered and mutilated the female members. The father, Harald Alexander, had decided that his sixteen year old son was 'a prophet ... inspired by God' and when he found his son beating his mother to death with a wooden coat-hanger in front of his two sisters he knew that 'the hour of killing had arrived' and set about attacking his daughters with a hammer. The girls didn't protest because they knew that their brother was 'the representative of God on earth'. When the father and son had finally killed the three women of their family they took turns in cutting their hearts out while the other played the organ. The hearts were then impaled on wooden stakes. When the remaining daughter of the family – who only avoided the same terrible fate by being out of the house at the time – was told of the horrific murders later, she clutched her father's hand and told him, 'I'm sure you've done what you thought necessary.' The motive for the attack we have already met before, as the father explained to the police: 'To be truly free, you must kill those whom you love more than anything else.' Again the same sentiment ... to be free you have to kill. It is a common thread running through the thinking of almost all of these mass murderers, particularly where religious obsession is concerned, and it is also a common thread running through the Bible. After all we are assured by John 1/2:15 as a general rule: 'Do not love the world or anything in the world.'

The last macabre case also shows convincingly that not all incidences of murder and mutilation are sexually related crimes, many of these brutal crimes in fact have their origins in religious doctrine. Alonzo Lopez, the mass murderer of Ecuador, explained it thus: 'The arrival of life is divine. It comes through the act of sex. And so if an innocent person dies in the act of sex, it is also divine. That person will find heaven without suffering in this world.'

Heinrich Pommerencke came away from the cinema in 1959 in Germany deeply influenced by the film he had just seen. It was 'The Ten Commandments' and he certainly underwent some kind of religious conversion because a few hours later he murdered and mutilated a woman. He told the police about the film he had seen: 'I saw half-naked women dancing around the golden calf. I thought then that many women were evil and did not deserve to live. I knew then I would have to kill.' 'The Amityville Horror' movie was based on the true story of Ronald De Feo who shot dead six members of his family while they slept. He claimed that he had shot all in self-defence. When asked why, he replied: 'I am God.'

Kidnapper and murderer Gary Heidnik had a long history of schizophrenia which turned to murder after he had had a 'revelation from God'. He founded his own church, made himself a bishop and when in court for multiple murder was never without his Bible.

Eric Chapman arrived at his Californian family home in July 1971 with a rifle in his hand. He informed his parents that as the 'second son of God' he was there to 'save them'. And how was Eric going to save them? By shooting them of course. Eventually he strangled his grandmother and was arrested as he tried to kill his parents again. When asked to explain his actions he responded:

> The Bible says to take a weapon and kill your parents ... Yeah, I told the police I had to kill my parents to be free. The Bible says to help them out, and they won't make you feel guilty anymore if they're dead ... my mother had a vase that proved I'm Jesus Christ, and when I was a child I broke the vase so they couldn't prove I wasn't Jesus Christ ... I resurrected her (the grandmother he strangled). I look a little like Him ... My accomplishment could save the world ... I'm Jesus.

When one reads through this terrible catalogue of murder and mutilation it is obvious that there are common factors involved in most of the crimes. Religious obsession is a dominating factor and so is the brutal treatment most of these killers suffered as children usually handed out by a mother. However, when the two are combined as we have seen in some of the worst cases, with an absent father through death or desertation, then it is a poisonous brew indeed. This is especially so when the mother is a religious fanatic who despises her biological self and teaches her son by the use of violence or brainwashing that sex, the sexual parts of women and women themselves are evil, sinful things with no place in the world. A child brought up thus is nothing less than a time bomb waiting to explode.

From the little we know of Thomas Cutbush it would seem that he was such a child. And when we look at the crimes of Jack the Ripper we can now see that they were committed by such a child as Thomas Cutbush.

The final question must be what exactly are these hordes of mass murderers and mutilators trying to tell us? Make no mistake they are not offering up apologies or excuses for mass murder, Panzram makes that quite clear: 'The only way to reform people is to kill them.' Ramirez makes it even clearer: 'See you in Disneyland.' Disneyland is Walt Disney's perfect world where religion doesn't exist, where all the mothers love their sons and evil is always conquered by good. Sex doesn't exist here so it isn't evil or sinful and there's no need to murder or mutilate anyone.

There is a coded message here for mankind but mankind has refused to acknowledge that message and until mankind does this very particular type of serial murder is bound to increase. Especially if we allow the modern-day prophets like Colin Wilson to lead us on the false path of believing that these mass murderers are sexual criminals seeking sexual satisfaction. It may suit Wilson to believe that but the truth of the matter is that these serial killers are symptomatic reactions to a system that still even today preaches that sex and the female body are evil. These killers have in fact an anti-sexual motive, they are killing 'sex'.

If we continue to teach our children that sex is somehow sinful and something to be punished, we will never be in a position to justifiably punish that child when he is an adult and brutally attacks that sin. Even when he commits mass murder and mutilates the reproductive organs of women, he is only fulfilling the role that society, the church and his family have programmed him for and the most disturbing aspect about mass murder is that Richard Ramirez was probably absolutely right when he said: 'Lucifer dwells in all of us.' But he may well have meant God.

And was Thomas Cutbush Jack the Ripper? Quite honestly it doesn't matter, for he is still out there walking the streets of Whitechapel …

Sources, References and Notes

Much of the Ripper story is such common knowledge today that it is not necessary to source every incident. However, where important new or contentious material is quoted the sources are given. A good deal of the published material relating to the Ripper story is presented by the authors without any sources or references and this allows the various theories of these authors to remain unchallenged. One is unable to either confirm or dispute their works because they do not make the facts available. This writer has extensively studied the available material related to the Ripper case in preparing this volume but sadly much of it cannot be used as source material because it cannot be challenged. For instance there seems to be no point in mentioning the books and papers that exploit the theory that Jack the Ripper was a murderous midwife when we now know that these same books were built on the single fact that Mary Jane Kelly was pregnant when murdered. We now know she was not. This is probably true for at least 50 per cent of all the Ripper material.

1 *Jack the Ripper*

1 Colin Wilson, *Written in Blood*, London 1990

2 & 3 Colin Wilson (with Robin Odell) *Jack the Ripper*, London 1988

4 Gordon Honeycombe, *The Murders of the Black Museum*, London 1982

5,6,7 & 8 Colin Wilson, *Mammoth Book of True Crime 2*, London 1990

9 A detailed report on the death of Mary Jane Kelly can be found in *Jack the Ripper A-Z*, Begg, Fido & Skinner, London 1991

10 Begg, Fido & Skinner, *Jack the Ripper A-Z*, London 1991

11 For an extensive summary and dismissal of Stephen Knight's theory *The Complete Jack the Ripper*, Donald Rumbelow, London 1988 is recommended

2 *Dorset Street*

1 There are still many who remain convinced that Peter Sutcliffe was not in fact the Yorkshire Ripper but a 'copy-cat' killer, and that police came to an arrangement with him to 'clear their books' in exchange for what was supposed to be an easy sentence. For a remarkable, if at times somewhat incoherent, account read *The Real Yorkshire Ripper Revealed*, Noel O'Gara (printed privately and full of errors but still with some interesting evidence)

2 In fairness it should be pointed out that both Stephen Knight and Gordon Honeycombe did realize the importance of Dorset Street to the Ripper crimes but failed to point their investigations in any useful direction

3 Paul Begg, *Jack the Ripper*: The Uncensored Facts, London 1990. But see below (No. 4) for an extensive summary of the Victorian London slums of Whitechapel and their occupants

4 Kellow Chesney, *The Victorian Underworld*, London 1970

5 Begg, Fido & Skinner, *The Jack the Ripper A-Z*, London 1991

6,7 & 8 Kellow Chesney, *The Victorian Underworld*, London 1970

9 Gordon Honeycombe, *Murders of the Black Museum*, London 1990

10 Kellow Chesney, *The Victorian Underworld*, London 1970

11 R. Pearsall, *The Worm in the Bud*, London

12 MEPO 3/140.262, Scotland Yard File, 18 July 1889, PRO Kew

13 Colin Wilson, *Jack the Ripper*, London 1988

14 Walter Dew, *I Caught Crippen*, London 1938

15 Again in fairness it should be pointed out that Stephen Knight also believed that all the Ripper's victims were known to one another. However he is the single exception

3 *Long Liz*

1 *Manchester Guardian*, 2 October 1888

2 *Manchester Guardian*, 2 October 1888

3 Begg, Fido & Skinner, *Jack the Ripper A-Z*, London 1991

4 *Evening News*, 1 October 1888
5 Home Office file, HO-144-220-A49301.C.8a, 19 October 1888
6 Home Office file (Scotland Yard origin), MEPO 3/140,26-28. Sir Charles Warren, Metropolitan Police Commissioner, affirms in these notes that he believes the man attacking Liz Stride called out 'Lipski!' to the witness Schwartz
7 Begg, Fido & Skinner, *Jack the Ripper A-Z*, London 1991
8 Rumbelow in his *The Complete Jack the Ripper* claims that Michael Kidney went to the police station after identifying Liz Stride's body. But he offers no source for his information. This is highly unlikely as on the same day that Kidney appeared at Leman Street police station Liz Stride had been identified as no less than four different women: Elizabeth Stokes/Annie Fitzgerald/Annie Morris and Wally Warden and some newspapers were still confused about her identity as late as 4 October and even 10 October. The inquest into her death was unusually long just because of the confusion about her identity (the inquest took place on the 1, 2, 3, 5 and 23 October). A Mary Malcolm appeared twice to swear that the deceased was her sister, Elizabeth Stokes, and it wasn't until the much later appearance of Mary Malcolm's sister, in the flesh, that the inquest jury were satisfied that she had misidentified the body. The first reference to Michael Kidney actually testifying to the inquest is in the *Daily News* 6 October, five days after he had complained to the police

4 Motives in the Dark

1 Colin Wilson, *Written in Blood*, London 1990
2 Colin Wilson, *Jack the Ripper*, London 1988
3 For an account of Peter Sutcliffe and his crimes see *Somebody's Husband, Somebody's Son*, London 1990 by Gordon Burn
4 Colin Wilson, *Jack the Ripper*, London 1988
5 Colin Wilson, *Written in Blood*, London 1990
6 Shere Hite, The Hite Report, London 1990
7, 8, 9, 10 & 11 Colin Wilson, *Mammoth Book of True Crime*, London 1988
12 Colin Wilson (with Robin Odell), *Jack the Ripper: Summing Up and Verdict*, London 1988
13 Shere Hite, The Hite Report on Male Sexuality, London 1990
14 Begg, Fido & Skinner, *Jack the Ripper A-Z*, London 1991
15 Colin Wilson, *The Mammoth Book of True Crime 2*, London 1990
16 All quotations in this book from the Bible are taken from the *Holy Bible: New International Version*, 1990
17 O.R. Gurney, *The Hittites*, London 1990

18 Homosexual rape and its horrifying consequences for the Ancient Egyptians has its origins in one of the oldest legends of man, the Osiris Myth in which Seth and Horus battle for the crown of Egypt and Seth rapes Horus while he sleeps. See *Myth and Symbol in Ancient Egypt* by R.T. Rundle Clark, London 1991

19 Colin Wilson, *Jack the Ripper*, London 1888

20 The authors of *Jack the Ripper A-Z*, Begg, Fido & Skinner

21 Dr Houchin, Medical Report, Colney Hatch Lunatic Asylum, Admissions and Discharges

5 *Sacrificial Lambs*

1 *The Times*, 10 November 1888

2 *The Times*, 10 November 1888

3 G. Vermes, *The Dead Sea Scrolls in English*, London 1990. The author is well aware that the 'Temple Scroll' was not discovered until 1956 and not read before 1967. However the slaughter ritual is exactly matched to that described in Exodus and Leviticus and also forms part of the strong oral traditions of the Talmud

6 *Suspects*

1 Begg, Fido & Skinner, *Jack the Ripper A-Z*, London 1991

2 Begg, Fido & Skinner, *Jack the Ripper A-Z*, London 1991

3 *News of the World*, 'Ripper haunted my life', 13 May 1984

4 Ambrahamsen, *Murder and Madness: The Secret Life of Jack the Ripper*, London 1992

5 M. Fairclough, *The Ripper and the Royals*, London 1992

6 Colin Wilson, *Written in Blood*, London 1990

7 & 8 Markman, Ronald (with Bosco), *Alone With the Devil*, London 1991

7 *Elimination*

1 Colin Wilson, *Mammoth Book of True Crime 2*, London 1990

2 Macnaghten paper, MEPO 3/141, Scotland yard File, PRO Kew

3 Sir Robert Anderson, *The Lighter Side of My Official Life*, London 1910

4 Major Henry Smith, *Constable to Commissioner: The Story of Sixty Years, Most of Them Misspent*, London 1910

5 Home Office File, HO-144-221-A49301. K, 11 September 1889

6 *Daily Telegraph*, 13 November 1888

8 Thomas Cutbush

1 Paul Begg, *Jack the Ripper*, London 1990

2 MEPO 3/141, Scotland Yard File, PRO Kew
3 MEPO 3/141, Scotland Yard File, PRO Kew
4 MEPO 3/141/259-262, Scotland Yard File, PRO Kew
5 *The Times*, 1 October 1888
6 Anderson, Sir Robert, *The Lighter Side of my Official Life*, London 1910
7 *The Times*, 12 October 1888

9 *Thomas: A Lonely Boy?*

1 *Sun*, 13, 14, 15, 16, 17, 18 & 19 February 1894, London
2 For the full story of the 'Vampire of Sacramento' see *Alone with the Devil*, Richard Markman, London 1991

Index